New Technologies in
Language Learning

Arne Zettersten

New Technologies in Language Learning

PERGAMON PRESS
OXFORD · NEW YORK · TORONTO · SYDNEY · FRANKFURT

UK
Pergamon Press., Headington Hill Hall,
Oxford OX3 OBW, England

USA
Pergamon Press Inc., Maxwell House, Fairview Park,
Elmsford, New York 10523, U.S.A.

CANADA
Pergamon Press Canada Ltd., Suite 104,
150 Consumers Road, Willowdale, Ontario M2J 1P9, Canada

AUSTRALIA
Pergamon Press (Aust.) Pty. Ltd., P.O. Box 544
Potts Point, N.S.W. 2011, Australia

FEDERAL REBUBLIC OF GERMANY
Pergamon Press GmbH, Hammerweg 6,
D-6242 Kronberg-Taunus, Federal Republic of Germany

Library of Congress Cataloging in Publication Data
Zettersten, Arne:
New technologies in language learning.
Includes index.
1. Languages, Modern-Study and teaching-Audiovisual aids. 2. Languages, Modern-Computer-assisted instruction. 3. Educational technology. I. Title.
LB1578.Z47 1986 407 85-25873

British Library Cataloguing in Publication Data
Zettersten, Arne:
New technologies in language learning.
1. Languages, Modern-Study and teaching
2. Educational innovations
I. Title
418'.007'8 PB36
ISBN 0-08-033888-7

Printed in Denmark 1986

220179

Preface

This survey of the use of new technologies in language learning is directed to anyone interested in new aspects of language acquisition, teachers, students, language planners, prospective writers of software, parents, administrators or those concerned with the future of education.

Writing a book on new technologies in education requires up-to-date information and good advice from numerous sources. I have been fortunate enough to obtain both from universities, libraries, publishers, colleagues and friends.

For useful information and advice I am indebted to John Trim and Eric Brown, Centre for Information on Language Teaching, London, Martin Phillips, British Council, London, Graham Davies, Ealing College, Tim Johns, University of Birmingham, Randall Jones, Brigham Young University, Provo, Utah, Earl Rand and Michael Cohen, University of California, Los Angeles, Udo Jung, University of Marburg, Bengt Sigurd, University of Lund, Mats Jacobson, Studentlitteratur AB, Lund, Claus Færch, English Department, University of Copenhagen, Margareta Broberg, Danmarks Pædagogiske Bibliotek, Copenhagen, and Morten Jønsson, Audio-Visual Department, University of Copenhagen.

In the English Department, University of Copenhagen, I also received valuable assistance from Gregory Stephenson in creating some model exercises, and in reading the proofs by Karen Kongsted, Gerd Bloxham, and Chris Tinson.

My thanks are also due to staff members of the following publishers: Liber, Malmö, Studentlitteratur AB, Lund, Gyldendal, Copenhagen, and Pergamon Press, Oxford.

Contents

Chapter 1

Can our present language training methods be improved on? Views on the future

The main purpose of this book is to give practical examples of how the newest technologies can be utilized in language learning. It is quite obvious that modern technology has developed very fast in recent years. At the same time it is quite amazing how slow educationalists have been in exploiting the capabilities of modern technology. One typical example is the rapid expansion of the microcomputer industry in the late seventies and early eighties compared to the slow advance of educational programs based on microcomputers (homecomputers).

Mainframe computers and minicomputers have admittedly been used a great deal for numerous educational purposes, but when the microchip revolution occurred and homecomputers started to inundate the market in many countries, teachers and educational theorists did not react with enough imagination and enthusiasm.

As in the case of the video boom of the seventies, young people took an enormous interest in the new technological gadgets but did not use them for educational purposes, simply because no-one gave them the opportunity to do so. Renting video films and playing video games became immensely popular in the seventies and continues to be so, just as using homecomputers for computer games became an obsession with many young people a little later in the seventies and in the eighties. The software production in the educational field is far from comparable to the hardware expansion. It is hoped that this book will help to close the gap between the technologically feasible and the educationally desirable, and will aid in effecting the enhancement of modern language learning through the appropriate use of the newest information and communication technologies.

Since I have used a variety of technologies for language training and language testing in recent years, I shall insert extracts and results from programs and tests and discuss advantages and disadvantages in each chapter of this book. There are numerous books and articles on the market explaining how microcomputers can be used in education. Some of these deal with language applications. Very few authors, however, have as yet attempted to give an overall survey of the possibilities of modern technology in language learning.

The practical approach which I have envisaged here, is directed to all individuals, students and teachers who intend to learn foreign languages or to help others to do so.

One of the main reasons for giving many practical examples of the programs and tests is that this will increase the possibility of discussing methodology and the possibility of future developments in foreign language acquisition.

Another reason is simply that the many handbooks and manuals dealing with new technology tend to be too technical and discuss hardware rather than software applications.

Considering all of the new technologies as a whole – how can our present language training methods best be improved? One answer to this question is a very important one. It is the one stating that exercises using new technologies should be regarded as complements or auxiliary aids to a language teacher and not as a replacement of his role. A technical device, a computer or a robot will never replace an efficient, well-trained language teacher. In some of the highly developed industrial countries, such as Japan, the USA, the Federal Republic of Germany, Sweden, Great Britain and France, industrial robots have taken over some of the monotonous chores, like spraypainting and spot-welding. In sectors such as transport and engineering robots are particularly useful. In Sweden, which has the highest density of industrial robots, there are about 30 robots for every 10,000 workers. It is, however, important to emphasize that these robots are used to perform monotonous jobs. In the same way, some of the technical aids in language training should be used exclusively for tasks where they will relieve the teacher of certain types of basic exercises so that he or she can find more time for communicative training. With the present level of technical advances it is fairly safe to hold the view that a live person is still the best teacher of communication. When it comes to certain basic skills, on the other hand, it may be debatable whether a personal computer or a videodisc may not be better than a teacher in a class-room situation. Futhermore, there are some combinations of techniques, for example a microcomputer and a video, from which a teacher might get enormous relief.

The actual improvements in methods will be found, among other things, in an increasing awareness among teachers that some of the basic training can be taken over by machines, so that the more interesting and more demanding task of communicative training in real-life situations can be refined to a much greater extent and to a much higher level. This question of the balance between basic knowledge and oral proficiency – between accuracy and fluency – will be discussed in Chapter 2.

The appropriate use of new technologies, the increasing awareness of the role of the machines, and consequently more time for communication exercises with preferably a functional/ notional approach are three areas of vital importance for the future development of language learning. I do not foresee any dramatic innovation in the methodology of teaching that will make the learning speed appreciably greater in the future. Some recent studies of the functions of the different areas of the brain indicate that some improvements can be predicted with more intensified research. There are also possibilites for improving the memorizing of words and structures. The increasing awareness of language learning processes will certainly prove most useful to both individuals and to language teachers. But the great leaps ahead will undoubtedly come through the use of adequate technologies in language learning.

As an introduction I shall present a few examples of how the technologies may provide quick access to large data-bases, specialized computerized dictionaries, diagnostic videotext tests, reinforcement microcomputer programmes, telesoftware, videodisc programmes, and many other innovations that can greatly facilitate learning. The following examples are only a fraction of those that will be discussed later:

1. The access to large data-bases includes not only useful data banks for research, such as the Brown University Corpus, the Lancaster-Oslo-Bergen Corpus, the Lund Corpus, and others, but also material stored on viewdata (videotext), such as Gyldendal's Encyclopedia in

Denmark, and various types of material stored on Prestel in Britain. Such data-bases will be indispensable for translators, business companies, LSP teachers and others.

2. The use of microcomputers for testing and training in languages could be expanded considerably if more software were available. Microcomputers (home computers) can be applied to a variety of functions, such as training grammar, vocabulary, content analysis, as well as many other aspects of language learning and testing.

3. The evolution and application of Viewdata/Videotext is only just starting in most countries. It can be applied to language training and testing.

4. New technologies in TV transmission will increase the possibility of quicker access to authentic material and will improve testing techniques. Teletext can be utilized for information and testing purposes. The increased use of satellite TV, cable TV, etc., will facilitate international communication and provide better access to relevant authentic language material.

5. The video techniques (the videodisc, etc.) will increase the possibilities of simulation exercises in language learning, and also increase the authenticity of illustrations of communicative teaching.

6. Synthetic speech has only a very marginal effect on language learning programmes though in particular cases it can be effectively used as a complementary device.

All these techniques and several others as well are applicable in various degrees to language learning situations. Some are useful for testing and distance education, some for applications in training business English or interpreting, some for primary schools, some for individual training at home. The teaching principle should be to appreciate new technologies in the areas and functions where they provide something decisively new and useful, and never let the machines take over the role of the teacher, or infringe on functions where more traditional ways are superior.

A counter-argument in this context is often heard. We had a kind of technological up-swing in the 1960's with a marked interest in language technology, language laboratories and programmed teaching. The boom of the 60's has not continued and, in fact, many people are tired of language laboratories, and teachers leave them unused or little used in many schools. So, why have another technology outburst, even though it may be on a much more advanced level than the previous one?

There are several answers to this counter-argument:

1. We know now that the machines should not be allowed to dominate too much in the process of learning languages.

2. We have a fuller picture of language learning as a process consisting of numerous components of which communicative faculties are very important ones.

3. We are in a position to learn from previous mistakes.

4. Some of the computer-based programs for language learning that were developed in the 1960's and 70's on mainframe computers illustrate the difference between that period and the 1980's after the microcomputer revolution. Computer techniques have become much more individualized and much less expensive.

5. Many people, particularly the young, have become much more technically-minded. There are no longer any inhibitions concerning the use of microcomputers or other electronic novelties among the average learners.

6. The diversity of this new technology makes the contrast to the 1960's astonishingly great.

There are various other reasons why it is important for all language learners to know about and make use of new technology. It suffices here to emphasize that new technologies now seem to develop and to be disseminated so quickly that their attraction and influence in one form or another is unavoidable. If one neglects or ignores them, developments will continue and one may never be able to catch up, irrespective of one's speciality or discipline. Even if electronic equipment is more important to scientists than it is to language learners, there is a strong need to be aware of the best and most modern equipment and to have maximum knowledge of what is suitable and available.

Chapter 2

The balance between accuracy and fluency.
The communicative approach.
The concepts of language functions and notions.
New technologies and basic needs

One of my theses in this book is to advocate that the balance between accuracy and fluency is one of the key issues in second language learning. A parallel thesis is that the new technologies are particularly relevant with a view to this relationship.

The balance between accuracy and fluency has been discussed by, for example, van Ek (1975), Brumfit (1981, 1984) and Roberts (1982), but also implicitly by several others. It is an interesting fact that scholars using various concepts for accuracy and fluency in language learning have stressed and given evidence of the contrast, and sometimes even the conflict, between accuracy and fluency. Some of these contrasting concepts are listed below and will be further discussed in order to prove the importance of the role of new technologies in language learning.

  I. Traditional Method Approach versus Communicative Approach. Cf. Strevens (1980), Roberts (1982).
 II. Norm-Oriented versus Performance-Oriented Language Teaching. Cf. Roberts (1982).
III. Formal/Grammatical versus Functional/Notional. Cf. van Ek (1976), Wilkins (1976).
 IV. Competence versus Performance. Cf. Canale-Swain (1980).
  V. Usage versus Use. Cf. Widdowson (1978).
 VI. Sentence Grammar versus Discourse Analysis. Cf. Widdowson (1973), Sinclair-Coulthard (1975), Halliday-Hassan (1976).
VII. Learning versus Acquisition. Cf. Krashen (1981, 1982). See, however, Dulay–Burt–Krashen (1982), where the terms *conscious* and *subconscious* language development are used instead.

VIII. Classroom teaching versus Real-life Contexts, authentic materials. Cf. Widdowson (1978), Strevens (1980).

  IX. Language-Centred Teaching versus Task-Centred Problem Solving, Simulation, Combinatory Acquisition. Cf. Maley (1983).

   X. Textbook versus Modules, Supplementary Materials, Station Systems of Learning.

In the first three concepts mentioned above (I-III), accuracy is associated with those traditional methods that are norm-oriented and based on learning formal grammar. This applies to the grammar-translation method as well as the pattern-drill method under which the structures are learnt in a fixed order, from the least to the most difficult ones. To a certain extent, this norm-orientation and formality with a focus on accuracy prevailed throughout the 1960's, despite the fact that language teaching became audio-lingual with more access to real-life situations.

Reflecting the change of interest towards more communication and greater stress given to performance analysis, a corresponding change in teaching materials and teaching syllabi also occurred. The increase in international travel and the wider access to TV films and to video programs have made oral production a more natural and relevant focal area than previously. The importance of training fluency to a greater degree has also been supported by theoretical discussions of language learning, such as, for example, the studies of competence versus performance (IV) and usage versus use (V), and the development of special projects for analysing discourse (VI).

One of the most rewarding results of the shift in emphasis to communicative teaching in the 1970's was the functional/notional approach to language learning as described by Wilkins (1976) and van Ek (1977). This approach is based on the assumption that communication can be regarded as a set of functions and notions which can be practised at various levels. The Council of Europe Language Project has devised a Threshold Level for communication which can be used as a starting point for exercises in communication. The method by which a video-programme based on a functional/notional approach can be planned, will be shown in Chapter 6.

Some of the areas for which language functions have been specified are the following:

16

1. Imparting and seeking factual information.
2. Expressing and discovering intellectual attitudes.
3. Expressing and discovering emotional attitudes.
4. Expressing and discovering moral attitudes.
5. Getting things done.
6. Socializing. Cf. van Ek (1976), 37-39.

One theory which has been strongly criticized e.g. by **K.R. Gregg** (*Applied Linguistics,* 5:2 (1984), pp. 79-100) but which may be discussed in terms of accuracy and fluency is Stephen Krashen's Monitor theory, described in Krashen (1981, 1982). According to Krashen a monitor mechanism governs and censors the process of language learning (VII.). This monitor, or editor, operates according to the consciously learned formal rules of the target language. The monitor operates successfully only under optimal and rather artificial conditions, such as classroom situations and examinations. It can tend to inhibit actual language performance. The process previously called *acquisition* by Krashen, on the other hand, is subconscious and enables the individual to store important information in his longterm memory without being censored by the monitor mechanism, and permits the retrieval of information when necessary. It is possible that the only contexts where there is a probability of finding a favourable environment for subconscious language development are real-life contexts in which fluency can be trained through task-centred problem solving exercises (VIII-IX). By combining language instruction and the teaching of other subjects, such as economics, for example, learners lose their inhibitions more easily and subconscious language development can take place. I have used the term *combinatory acquisition* to indicate instances when language is acquired in combination with a totally different discipline. Examples of this principle will be provided in Chapters 6 and 7.

In order to fulfill the wealth of new requirements of language learners, new types of instructional materials have been and continue to be developed (X). If both accuracy and fluency are to be reflected in the teaching materials, then it is obvious that great diversity of approach will be required. It is clear that the new technologies will create a need for even greater diversity in the supplementary material. My view is that both accuracy and fluency must be regarded as complementary and co-equal aspects of the language learning process, and that both must be given suitable attention if the language is to be learnt properly. The various new technologies which are described in this book afford the possibility of improving both accuracy and fluency, each in its own manner.

The early generations of programs based on new technologies were devised to increase accuracy to a much greater extent than they were designed to improve fluency. To a degree, this limitation is inherent in the nature of the medium, for it is highly doubtful whether a technical device, a machine or robot will ever replace a good teacher for the practice of oral communication. There are, on the other hand, particular basic needs as regards both accuracy and fluency where the new technologies are appropriate and effective. Perhaps their greatest advantage is that they relieve the language teacher of tedious or repetitious tasks and thereby enable him or her to concentrate on the communicative aspects of language learning, a more challenging and more rewarding undertaking, and one for which the teacher should be uniquely qualified.

In self-study as well, there is a need for greater diversity in learning methods and in supplementary materials. The new technologies will be very important sources for new ideas and approaches to individualized study and will be capable of meeting the need for such diversity. Indeed, the existence of these technologies will greatly facilitate the improvement of both accuracy and fluency at every level of application. There is every reason to hope that the new technologies may at last resolve the issue of accuracy and fluency, so that, in time, accuracy may become more fluent, and fluency more accurate.

Chapter 2: **Sources and further reading**

Brazil, D./ Coulthard, M. /Johns, C. (1980), *Discourse Intonation and Language Teaching*. London: Longman.

Brumfit, C.J. (1981), "Accuracy and fluency: a fundamental distinction for communicative teaching methodology", *Practical English Teacher*, I:3.

Brumfit, C.J./ Johnson, K. (1979), *The Communicative Approach to Language Teaching*. London: Oxford University Press.

Brumfit, C.J. (1984), *Communicative Methodology in Language Teaching: the Roles of Fluency and Accuracy*. Cambridge: Cambridge University Press.

Canale, M./ Swain, M. (1980), "Theoretical Bases of Communicative Approaches to Second Language Teaching and Testing", *Applied Linguistics,* I, pp. 1-47.

Coulthard, M. (1977), *An Introduction to Discourse Analysis.* London: Longman.

Dulay, H./ Burt, M./ Krashen, S. (1982), *Language Two.* New York: Oxford University Press.

van Ek, J. (1975), *The Threshold Level in a European Unit/Credit System for Modern Language Learning by Adults.* Strasbourg: Council of Europe.

van Ek. J. (1976), *Significance of the Threshold Level in the Early Teaching of Modern Languages.* Strasbourg: Council of Europe.

van Ek, J. (1977), *The Threshold Level for Modern Language Learning in Schools.* London: Longman.

Færch, C./ Haastrup, K./ Phillipson, R. (1984), *Learner Language and Language Learning.* Copenhagen: Gyldendal and Multilingual Matters Ltd.

Halliday, M./ Hassan, R. (1976), *Cohesion in English.* London: Longman.

Hatch, Evelyn M. (1983), *Psycholinguistics. A Second Language Perspective.* Rowley, Mass.: Newbury House.

Knapp-Potthoff, A./Knapp, K. (1982), *Fremdsprachenlernen und -lehren.* Stuttgart: Kohlhammer.

Krashen, S. (1981), *Second Language Acquisition and Second Language Learning.* Oxford: Pergamon Press.

Krashen, S. (1982), *Principles and Practice in Second Language Acquisition.* Oxford: Pergamon Press.

Krashen, S./ Terrell, T. (1983), *The Natural Approach.* Oxford: Pergamon Press.

Maley, A. (1983), "New lamps for old: realism and surrealism in foreign language teaching", *ELT Journal,* Vol. 37/4, October, pp. 295-303.

McDonough, S.H. (1981), *The Psychology of Foreign Language Learning.* London: George Allen and Unwin.

Richards, J.C./Schmidt, R.W. (1983), *Language and Communication.* London: Longman.

Roberts, J.T. (1982), "Recent developments in ELT", Part I and Part II, *Language Teaching,* April 1982, pp. 94-110, July 1982, pp. 174-94.

Sinclair, J.M./ Coulthard, M. (1975), *Towards an analysis of discourse: the English used by teachers and pupils.* London: Oxford University Press.

Strevens, P. (1980), *Teaching English as an International Language – from practice to principle.* Oxford: Pergamon Press.

Widdowson, H.G. (1973), "Directions in the teaching of discourse", in Corder, S.P./ Roulet, E., eds., *Theoretical Linguistics Models in Applied Linguistics.*

Widdowson, H.G. (1978), *Teaching Language as Communication.* Oxford: Oxford University Press.

Wilkins, David A. (1976), *Notional syllabuses: a taxonomy and its relevance to foreign language curriculum development.* London: Oxford University Press.

Chapter 3

Microcomputers in language learning:
Grammar, vocabulary,
spelling, pronunciation, authoring systems

The aim of this chapter is to give some practical examples of how microcomputers could be used in second language learning. There are numerous books on the market explaining the applications of the microcomputer, for example, C. Evans (1979), *The Mighty Micro;* L. Malone – J. Johnson (1981), *BASIC Discoveries;* and A. Luehrmann – H. Peckham – M. Ramirez (1982), *A First Course in Computing.* There are also some recent works dealing with microcomputers in education, such as P. Coburn, et al. (1982), *Practical Guide to Computers in Education;* T. O'Shea – J. Self (1983), *Learning and Teaching with Computers;* J. Higgins – T. Johns (1984), *Computers in Language Learning,* K. Ahmad, et al. (1985), *Computers, Language Learning and Language Teaching,* and J. Self (1985), *Microcomputers in Education.*

As regards computers, we are now dealing with the fourth and fifth generations. There has been constant improvement. The development of hardware and the competition among producers of hardware have been extremely intensive in the seventies and eighties. As for the corresponding software production in language training, I think it is justifiable to characterize it as the first generation of language learning programs. Software producers have been slow to produce "courseware", particularly in the area of language learning. It may well be that the second generation of CALL (= Computer-Assisted Language Learning) technology, which is currently being developed, will cause software producers to achieve a degree of parity with hardware manufacturers in the race for prospective buyers. It is also to be hoped that the various computer literacy programs which are being instituted in many countries will eventually lead to greater knowledge and awareness among individual users so that programming can attain much wider dissemination and achieve much faster and higher development.

Computer-assisted instruction (=CAI) has operated for many years on both mainframe computers and minicomputers. The best known CAI system on mainframe computers is PLATO, a system which was developed at the University of Illinois in the 1960's. Over the years a great amount of excellent software has been produced, also for the purpose of language learning. It is interesting to note that the PLATO courses which, because of their cost, have been used by business companies, universities, and large organizations, are currently also available for use on home computers.

There are also terminal-based CAI systems operating with the aid of minicomputers. The best known system is probably TICCIT, which was developed by Brigham Young University, Utah, where programs for learning German have been produced.

At present there is also a Micro TICCIT, which is a multimedia system incorporating features such as videodiscs, videotape, random access digital stored audio, student interaction via touch or light pen, as well as other features.

There is a variety of ways in which the individual user or the student in a learning situation can employ the new technology offered by microcomputers. The following situations are the most common ones:

1. The user may buy the CALL programs available on the market for his own personal computer. This would also apply to schools, business companies and organizations responsible for language training.

2. A user or a teacher, even without any knowledge of computer programming, can make exercises much more individualized by using the so-called *authoring programs*. Such programs are specifically designed for particular learning areas, such as grammar, vocabulary, translation, multiple-choice tests, cloze tests, etc. See, for example, BRAINLEARN, fig. 2, p. 40.

3. The individual teacher who has learnt programming may prefer to create his own programs, perhaps in conjunction with the use of existing software mentioned under 1 and 2.

21

In this chapter some practical examples of the contents of language exercises on microcomputers will be given. An example of the actual design of an authoring program will be provided in an appendix (pp. 159-66).

Most of the existing language training programs for the microcomputer are exercises which are based on the assumption that certain skills can be trained in isolation. Such exercises have been called drill-and-practice programs (Higgins-Johns) and are usually gap-filling exercises, that is, exercises in which the user provides the missing element in the sentence.

Naturally, there are both advantages and disadvantages to such programs. Reinforcing grammatical and lexical skills by microcomputers has proved to be most effective in some of the test schools chosen in the Swedish evaluation project carried out in 1983-85. No doubt some exercises are more meaningful than others. Higgins and Johns point out that "when the computer itself generates the practice material, the resulting exercise may be in essence a meaningful drill." (p. 39). The generative approach is not, however, the only one which can result in meaningful language learning experiences. If sufficient variety and imagination are brought to bear upon the planning of a set of exercises for a particular grammatical item the effect of reinforcement can be greatly enhanced. A few examples of some different types of exercises dealing with pronouns will be given below. First a few pictures from the *beginning* of a program with gap-filling exercises will be shown.

1.

THIS IS HOW THE PROGRAM WORKS
In each of the following sentences there is a blank where a pronoun is missing. Write in the word that best fits the sentence.
Example: He is the only person ..... opinion I respect.
Press RETURN

2.

The right answer is: *whose*
He is the only person *whose* opinion I respect.
Press RETURN

3.

* The computer will tell you if your answer is right or wrong.
* To have a good practice session you should do about 50 sentences.
* When you finish write down the number of right answers you gave or ask for a print-out.
* If your score is not very high, take a break and then try again.

Press RETURN

4.

* You can change your answer (correct your spelling errors) before you press RETURN. To do this you must use the BACK key, which is located at the extreme right of the keyboard.
* You can stop the exercise by pressing F (=FINISH).
* You can go on to the next picture by pressing C (=CONTINUE).
* You can read the instructions again by pressing I (=INSTRUCTIONS).

Press RETURN.

In order to show how a contrastive approach can be used, some examples of the data belonging to an exercise practising indefinite pronouns are given below. In every picture a Swedish sentence is given first, followed by the corresponding English sentence with a gap for the pronoun in question. A brief grammar rule is provided together with the correct sentence in English.

1.

(1) Något underligt hände mig häromdagen.
..... strange happened to me the other day.
Svar: something
some med sammansättningar används i påståendesatser.
Rätt mening: Something strange happened to me the other day.

2.

Jag köpte några bra böcker på bokrean.
I bought ..... good books at the book sales.
Svar: some
some med sammansättningar används i påståendesatser.
Rätt mening: I bought some good books at the book sales.

23

3.

Någon måste ha lånat honom pengarna.

..... must have lent him the money.

Svar: somebody, someone

Någon (om person) utan något substantiv som följer heter *somebody* eller *someone* i påståendesatser.

Rätt mening: Somebody (Someone) must have lent him the money.

4.

Vi kunde inte se någonting.

We couldn't see .....

Svar: anything

any med sammansättningar används i frågande och nekande satser.

Rätt mening: We couldn't see anything.

5.

Vi har inte hört någonting från honom än.

We haven't heard ..... from him yet.

Svar: anything

any med sammansättningar används i frågande och nekande satser.

Rätt mening: We haven't heard anything from him yet.

6.

Ingen kan hjälpa honom.

..... can help him.

Svar: nobody, no one

ingen (om person) utan något följande substantiv heter *nobody* eller *no one*.

Rätt mening: Nobody (No one) can help him.

The next program deals with interrogative pronouns.

Fill in the blanks in the following sentences using *who, whose, whom* or *which*.

1. The man _____ spoke to me is John's father.
2. The woman _____ book you are reading is a friend of mine.
3. The magazines _____ are on the table belong to me.
4. The boy did not know to _____ he should give the flowers.

5. I feel sorry for people _____ must go to bed hungry each night.
6. This is the house in _____ I lived for three years.
7. Mary, _____ is a good dancer, will be performing tonight.

The following is a contrastive program (Danish – English) dealing with four different sorts of pronouns.

Fill in the missing English pronouns in the sentences below, using the Danish pronouns as a guide.

1. Are _____ your shoes?
   (disse)

2. _____ has stolen my car.
   (nogen)

3. _____ is your favourite book?
   (hvilken)

4. Is _____ the one you're looking for?
   (dette)

5. There is _____ here.
   (ingen)

6. I don't think we have _____ to eat in the house.
   (noget)

7. _____ is the man in the blue coat?
   (hvem)

8. Has _____ seen my hat?
   (nogen)

9. _____ has gone on holiday.
   (alle)

10. There is _____ strange going on here.
    (noget)

In order to make the exercises even more diversified and to appeal to the imagination of the user, a game element can be introduced. An example of the structure of a game dealing with pronouns will be provided:

The Great English Pronoun Theft is a computer game designed to test and to teach proficiency in the use of five types of pronouns: demonstrative, relative, interrogative, possessive and indefinite.

Sequence of operations:
1. The student-operator reads the story of the Great English Pronoun Theft. (Pictures 1 and 2).
2. The student-operator reads the instructions for playing the game. (Picture 3).
3. The game consists of the testimonies of seven suspects. The testimonies lack pronouns, which the student must fill in. In one of the suspect's testimonies there is a clue which should alert the student to the identity of the "Pronoun Thief".
4. If at the end of the game the student has a sufficiently large score he/she may guess who the "Pronoun Thief" is. If the student's guess is incorrect, he/she may guess again until he/she guesses correctly.
5. If at the end of the game the student-operator's score is not high enough, he/she may repeat the game to attempt a higher score.

The Great English Pronoun Theft

1.

On an ordinary afternoon last week, the citizens of a small English town were shocked to discover that nearly all of their pronouns had been stolen. Demonstrative pronouns were completely gone. Relative, possessive and interrogative pronouns had all been taken. Not even a single indefinite pronoun had been left behind by the Pronoun Thief. Only personal pronouns had been overlooked, perhaps because the Pronoun Thief had not had time to take them, or perhaps because he didn't think them worth his trouble.

2.

The effect of the loss of their pronouns was devastating to the towns-people who could now only with difficulty understand each other. Inspector Syntax of the Royal Speech Police was called in on the case and he questioned seven suspects.

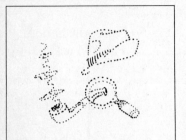

Fig. 1
Inspector Syntax

3.

You can help Inspector Syntax to discover who is behind the Great English Pronoun Theft by restoring the missing pronouns in the following statements made by suspects.

For each pronoun that you restore correctly you will receive one point. If your final score is above _____ points you will be allowed to guess which of the suspects is the Pronoun Thief.

If your score is under _____ points you may be suspected of being the Pronoun Thief yourself. But you can go back and try again for a higher score.

The following is a sample testimony of a suspect:

4.

The moment that I saw that man I thought to _____: "Oh, I don't like the look of _____. He was, you know, sort of sneaky-looking. Always smiling to _____ secretly, if you know what I mean."

5.

Correct answers:
  myself
  him
  himself

6.

The first thing he said to me was: "To _____ do I have the honour of speaking?" "You mean you want to know _____ I am?" I asked him. "Yes, _____ is correct," he said.

7.

Correct answers:
  whom
  who
  that

8.

I noticed that he was very careful about _____ speech. I thought maybe he was a foreigner _____ was trying to disguise his accent. And it was then that I realized that I couldn't find _____ pronouns. He'd taken _____.

9.

Correct answers:
  his
  who
  my, any
  them

Various types of test methods may be used in connection with verb exercises. A multiple choice test is a variant of a *question-answer dialogue* between the computer and the student. Examples of this will be given in Chapter 11. Such tests may be used as a diagnostic test to ensure that the student chooses the appropriate level of difficulty when starting the exercises. They may also be used at the end of an exercise period to ascertain if the necessary proficiency in the particular grammar area (pronouns, in this instance) has been attained.

The first example I shall provide is a contrastive exercise (Swedish-English) in which the correct form of the verb should be placed in the gap.

1.

Mr Greene har rest till Frankrike.
Mr Greene has ..... to France. (go)
Svar: gone   Tema: go – went – gone
Rätt mening: Mr Greene has gone to France.

2.

Vi reste till Tyskland.
We ..... to Germany. (go)
Svar: went   Tema: go – went – gone
Rätt mening: We went to Germany.

3.

Har Pat kommit hem än?
Has Pat ..... home yet? (come)
Svar: come   Tema: come – came – come
Rätt mening: Has Pat come home yet?

4.

Kent kom hem i går.
Kent ..... home yesterday. (come)
Svar: came   Tema: come – came – come
Rätt mening: Kent came home yesterday.

5.

Jag sov till klockan åtta.
I ..... until eight o'clock.
Svar: slept   Tema: sleep-slept-slept
Rätt mening: I slept until eight o'clock.

The following exercise is also contrastive (Danish-English). The student fills in the form of the verb in brackets that corresponds to the form of the verb in the Danish sentence.

1. Hun vidste godt at han var forbryder.
   She _____very well that he was a criminal.
   (know)

2. Han følte sig fortvivlet.
   He _____ confused.
   (feel)

3. De gik op ad trappen.
   They _____ up the stairs.
   (go)

4. Hun havde trukket ham til sig som en magnet.
   She had _____ him to her like a magnet.
   (draw)

5. Hun rejste sig og gik ud i byen.
   She _____ and walked to town.
   (rise)

6. Hun stod stille som var hun af sten.
   She _____ as still as if she were made of stone.
   (stand)

7. Han talte ganske roligt.
   He _____ quite calmly.
   (speak)

8. Han lå hulkende på sengen.
   He _____ sobbing on the bed.
   (lay)

9. Jeg er blevet mere klog siden dengang.
   I have _____ wiser since then.
   (become)

10. Han har fundet brevet.

   He has _____ the letter.

         (find)

The exercise that follows is a continuous story in which the Danish verb form is given below each gap, while the English verb in the infinitive form is given in brackets.

Since it was exotic scenery and new experiences that I ___(seek)___ , I decided

                                                     1. søgte

that I would ___(spend)___ some time in the Western United States.

                  2. tilbringe

  Every day I ___(spend)___ there, ___(bring)___ me some new and unexpected

             3. tilbragte   4. bragte

pleasure or adventure. First, I ___(fly)___ to New York and then ___(take)___

                            5. fløj   6. tog

a bus west. On my very first day in Arizona I ___(meet)___ a Navajo Indian in

                                      7. mødte

a restaurant and we hadn't ___(speak)___ for more than half an hour before he

                          8. talt

invited me to stay with him in his home.

  We ___(drive)___ for several kilometers down dirt roads that ___(bend)___

      9. kørte   10. bøjede

and ___(wind)___ around hills and mountains until we reached his small

    11. snoede (sig)

house, ___(build)___ of stones and animal hides.

     12. bygget

Finally, the first part of a story *(The Bandit)* in which only the English verb in the infinitive form is given.

I _____ on the cold ground in the darkness, and for a moment I

  1. (wake)

_____ that I had _____ and that I had _____ off my cot and

  2. (think)   3. (dream)   4. (fall)

had _____ my head on a rock or something. I _____ up and then

    5. (hit)   6. (stand)

quickly I _____ down to the ground again. My head _____

      7. (sink)   8. (hurt)

terribly, my ears _____ like a bell, and I _____ sick to my
             9. (ring)   10. (feel)

stomach. My mind _____ around and around, and a word _____
                  11. (spin)   12. (keep)

running through my head: gold, gold, gold. I _____ over to my canteen
                                      13. (creep)

and _____ a long swallow of cold water. I _____ owls calling in
    14. (take)   15. (hear)

the trees, it _____ late. But what _____ happened?
            16. (be)   17. (have)

  Then suddenly it all _____ back to me. Someone had _____ me
                  18. (come)   19. (strike)

while I _____, and then had _____ himself on me, and we had
       20. (sleep)   21. (fling)

_____ in the darkness. He _____ in Spanish when I _____
 22. (fight)   23. (swear)   24. (hit)

him and I had _____ the tequila on his breath. Obviously, he had
            25. (smell)

_____ the fight. And now my gold had been _____.
 26. (win)   27. (steal)

There are also methods of testing particular communicative functions by means of multiple choice tests, cloze tests or tests in which multiple choice and cloze exercises are combined. This latter alternative is, however, much more complicated than using either multiple choice or cloze tests exclusively. Some examples of communicative tests which may be used on the microcomputer can be found in P. Hellgren (1982) *Communicative Proficiency in a Foreign Language and its Evaluation,* pp. 160-64. For a discussion of communicative courseware, see D. Sanders-R. Kenner (1983), "Whither CAI? The Need for Communicative Courseware", *System*, 11:2, pp. 33-39.

Vocabulary

The microcomputer can also be utilized as an instrument for learning vocabulary. The advantage is that samples of words can be selected according to frequency and can be arranged on different levels of proficiency. A student can therefore begin at a modest level and increase the level of difficulty step-by-step. The examples given below are from a corpus of 10,000 different words representing the lowest and the highest levels corresponding to the expected proficiency in grades 4 to 6 (level 1), and grade 12 (level 7) in the Swedish school system. See F. Thorén (1967).

Level 1

1. always	2. jump	3. bad	4. kitchen
5. child	6. length	7. deep	8. mother
9. easy	10. nose	11. face	12. only
13. girl	14. perhaps	15. happy	16. roof
17. how	18. shop	19. if	20. table

Level 7

1. altitude	2. magnify	3. blackmail	4. nuisance
5. cardboard	6. overwhelm	7. compatriot	8. pedestrian
9. depressed	10. postpone	11. filth	12. referee
13. gravy	14. spine	15. hedgehog	16. tan
17. incredible	18. tickle	19. laundry	20. valve

The data from an exercise containing words from Level 2 (grade 7) could look like this (Swedish-English):

1.

Exercise 1 contains the following words:

cloud	bottom
length	wool
hero	lamp
skirt	truth
captain	heel

Translate into Swedish:

cloud	moln	(Rätt)
length	längd	(Rätt)
hero	hjälte	(Rätt)
skirt	kjol	(Rätt)
captain	kapten	(Rätt)

bottom	botten	(Rätt)
wool	ull	(Rätt)
lamp	lampa	(Rätt)
truth	sanning	(Rätt)
heel	häl, klack	(Rätt)

2.

Exercise 2 contains the following words:

holy	earth
among	air
wolf	knee
author	proud
lung	belong

Translate into Swedish:

holy	helig	(Rätt)
among	bland	(Rätt)
wolf	varg	(Rätt)
author	författare	(Rätt)
lung	lunga	(Rätt)
earth	jord	(Rätt)
air	luft	(Rätt)
knee	knä	(Rätt)
proud	stolt	(Rätt)
belong	tillhöra	(Rätt)

3.

Exercise 3 contains the following words:

thirsty	steal
shoot	cheese
breast	knowledge
glove	dare
calf	Danish

Translate into Swedish:

thirsty	törstig	(Rätt)
shoot	skjuta	(Rätt)
breast	bröst	(Rätt)
glove	handske	(Rätt)
calf	kalv	(Rätt)
steal	stjäla	(Rätt)
cheese	ost	(Rätt)
knowledge	kunskap	(Rätt)
dare	våga	(Rätt)
Danish	dansk	(Rätt)

If, in certain cases, several translations are possible, they must all be regarded as correct answers by the program.

Spelling exercises are also very effectively presented by means of a microcomputer. The simplest way is to ask the user to write individual words that are first shown briefly one by one on the screen. By letting the user choose his own speed and allowing him to compare his own results at different speeds, a game element can be introduced and make the exercises more appealing. See, for example, "Spellbound" in the Brainlearn system, p. 40. Alternatively, an audio unit can be used to pronounce individual words, after which the user writes in the correct spelling. The selection of words may be based on frequency studies, as in the case of vocabulary tests on microcomputers (see Ch. 11). On the basis of a similar selection procedure, the following example shows how words are selected from eight different frequency bands to be used in spelling programs. The relevant Swedish school level is indicated in brackets.

Level 1 (4-6)	Level 2 (7)	Level 3 (8)	Level 4 (9)
almost	across	abroad	accident
about	address	accept	accompany
above	allow	article	association
answer	arrival	attention	appearance
beautiful	believe	behaviour	bodyguard
beginning	building	borrow	breakfast
choose	catcher	carriage	ceaseless

children	ceiling	certainly	changeable
colour	collar	chairman	channel
coming	command	chalk	commit

Level 5	Level 6	Level 7	Level 8
(10)	(11)	(12)	(Univ.)
abolish	accumulate	acclamation	accomplice
abuse	accurate	acquit	acoustics
assault	ascend	ascertain	annihilate
available	attribute	assassinate	audible
boundary	bounteous	bristle	bulldozer
bough	bribery	burglar	cleavage
casing	cashier	celebrity	cartoon
carpentry	casual	character	chasm
caravan	caress	certify	calculation
cardinal	coexistence	celestial	compact

The words can either be practised in isolation or in context. Sentences similar to the following may be used to present the words in context. (These examples are from Level 8, for students with a vocabulary of approximately 10,000 words.)

1. I think the murderer had an *accomplice*.
2. The *acoustics* in the concert hall are perfect.
3. An atomic war would *annihilate* mankind.
4. The music was barely *audible* during the storm.
5. A *bulldozer* was used to clear the road of fallen trees.

The use of an audio unit helps significantly in making exercises more true-to-life. The linking of an audio recorder to a microcomputer is, however, only fully effective if a random-access function is available. Tandberg, Norway, has developed a new recorder with this function, which lends itself to a number of pronunciation exercises.

In order to practise minimal pairs, for example, the following type of exercise can be used:

1.

1. The sculpture was made of _____ and stone.
   (1) metal
   (2) medal

2.

(1) Good. Go on to the next question.
(2) Sorry. A medal is an award for excellence or achievement.

3.

2. The traffic consisted mainly of _____ and bicycles.
   (1) buzzes
   (2) buses

4.

(1) Sorry. Buzzes means a humming sound.
(2) Good. Go on to the next question.

5.

3. The scar on her _____ was caused by a childhood accident.
   (1) chin
   (2) gin

6.

(1) Good. Go on to the next question.
(2) Sorry. Gin is an alcoholic beverage.

7.

4. He is considered to be a _____ employee.
   (1) muddle
   (2) model

8.

(1) Sorry. Muddle means a state of confusion.
(2) Good. Go on to the next question.

9.

5. There is a _____ in the gas tank that is causing reduced mileage.
   (1) leak
   (2) league

10.

(1) Good. Go on to the next question.
(2) Sorry. A league is a type of association or a measure of distance.

There are many ways in which the use of microcomputers can be varied and further developed in addition to those that have already been suggested in this chapter. The use of audio devices, touch screens (i.e. touching the screen for input rather than using the keyboard), sound generators, speech synthesis, simulation and linking the micro-computer to other systems (telesoftware) will make computer-assisted language learning much more exciting and individualized, particularly when we have learnt how to adapt our knowledge of the hardware to the needs of the learner and to use our imagination to make the software more meaningful and effective.

It is a regrettable fact that all software in most countries is so new that few evaluation projects have been started. We do not know to what extent a particular group of students using language exercises with a microcomputer have acquired greater language proficiency than a comparable group not having used computers. Nor do we know as yet what type of acquisition the computer stimulates best. One observation, however, has been made by teachers taking part in the evaluation project initiated by the National Board of Education in Sweden. Slow learners, who may not always get enough stimulation in a classroom situation, seem to regard the individual speed of the computer as a great advantage. This observation is an important one, and it emphasizes the role of the microcomputer as a highly flexible instrument which can cater to individual needs to a much greater degree than has been thought possible so far.

One way of making exercises even more individual or user-specific is to use more computer-generated material. In programs which instruct the computer to generate adequate questions on the basis of interaction with the user, there is also a chance of making the user more active and creative. See Higgins-Johns, pp. 53-62.

One area which remains to be explored fully is the linking of microcomputers to a videodisc unit. Videodisc micros certainly open up new possibilities of training communicative functions and introducing exciting simulations. A discussion of video and videodiscs can be found in Chapter 6.

A new learning system for various modern languages was devised by Mats Jacobson and myself for Studentlitteratur, Lund, Sweden. This system, which was produced for the IBM PC, contains a series of readymade exercises dealing with text manipulation ("Textbrain"), vocabulary ("Wordbrain"), grammar, and spelling ("Spellbound"), as well as a series of "authoring programs", with which a company or school can write in or update special words and phrases as well as technical or economic texts. So far English and French exercises have been produced. The "authoring programs" in the system can, however, be applied to most languages with alphabetical script. The details of the various components of the Brainlearn system are displayed in fig. 2, p. 40. An example of how an authoring program is built up is given in a special appendix, pp. 159-66. The enormous advantage of using an authoring program is that the user ("author") can type in all instructions in plain language and does not have to use any special instructional symbols. The disadvantage is that the user is limited by the pedagogical system followed by the original programmer.

BRAINLEARN

A new learning system for English, German, French, etc.

by Arne Zettersten and Mats Jacobson

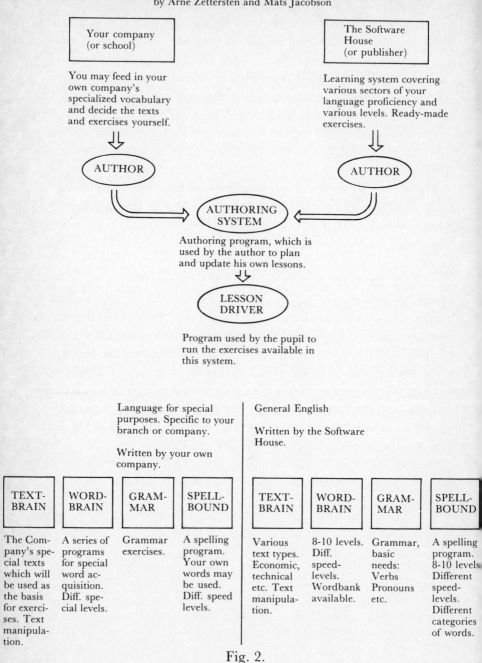

Fig. 2.

A *Computers*

Bradbeer, R./ De Bono, P./ Laurie, P. (1982), *The Computer Book: An Introduction to Computers and Computing*. London: BBC Publications.

Capron, H. L./ Willi, B.K. (1984), *Computers and Data Processing*. 2nd ed. Menlo Park, California: The Benjamin/Cunnings Publishing Co., Inc.

Evans, C. (1979), *The Mighty Micro*. London: Victor Gollancz.

Forester, T. (1980), *The Microelectronics Revolution*. Oxford: Basil Blackwell.

Helms, H. L., ed. (1983), *The McGraw-Hill Computer Handbook*. New York: McGraw-Hill.

Luehrmann, A./ Peckham, H./ Ramirez, M. (1982), *A First Course in Computing*. New York: McGraw-Hill.

Malone, L/ Johnson, J. (1981), *BASIC Discoveries*, Palo Alto, Ca.: Creative Publications.

Parker, Sibyl B., ed. (1984), *Encyclopedia of Electronics and Computers*. New York: McGraw-Hill.

B *Computers and education*

Arbib, M.A. (1984), *Computers and the Cybernetic Society*. 2nd ed. Orlando, Florida: Academic Press, Inc.

CAL News. London: Council of Educational Technology.

CET Information Sheets. London: Council of Educational Technology.

CET News. London: Council of Educational Technology.

Coburn, P. *et.al.* (1982), *Practical Guide to Computers in Education*. Reading, Mass.: Addison-Wesley Publishing Company.

Educational Computing. Haywards Heath, Sussex: MAGSUB Ltd.

Educational Media International. London: International Council for Educational Media.

Ellingham, D. (1982), *Managing the Microcomputer in the Classroom*. MEP Case Study, No. 1. London: Council for Educational Technology.

Hawkidge, D. (1983), *New Information Technology in Education*. London: Croom Helm.

Hockey, Susan (1980), *A Guide to Computer Applications in the Humanities*. Baltimore and London: Johns Hopkins University Press.

Howe, J.A.M./ Ross, P.M., eds. (1981), *Microcomputers in Secondary Education: Issues and Techniques*. London: Kogan Page.

Jones, R. (1980), *Microcomputers: Their Uses in Primary Schools*. London: Council of Educational Technology.

Lewis, B./ Tagg, D., eds. (1981), *Computers in Education*. Amsterdam: North Holland.

MEP Information Sheets. Newcastle upon Tyne: Microelectronics Education Programme.

Odor, P./ Entwistle, N. (1982), *The Introduction of Microelectronics into Education*. Edinburgh: Scottish Academic Press.

O'Shea, T./ Self, J. (1983), *Learning and Teaching with Computers*. Brighton: The Harvester Press.

Papert, S. (1980), *Mindstorms: Children, Computers and Powerful Ideas*. Brighton: The Harvester Press.

Rushby, N.J. (1979), *An Introduction to Educational Computing*. London: Croom Helm.

Self, J. (1985), *Microcomputers in Education*. Brighton: The Harvester Press.

Smith, C. (1982), *Microcomputer in Education*. London: Ellis Harwood/ John Wiley.

USPEC. London: Council of Educational Technology.

Weizenbaum, J. (1984), *Computer Power and Human Reason. From Judgment to Calculation*. Harmondsworth, Middlesex: Penguin Books Ltd.

C *Computers and language learning*

Ahmad, K., *et al.* (1985), *Computers, Language Learning and Language Teaching*. Cambridge: Cambridge University Press.

CALLBOARD: Newsletter on Computer Assisted Language Learning. London: Ealing College.

Calico Journal. Provo, Utah: Brigham Young University Press.

Chandler, D. (1983), *Exploring English with Microcomputers*. London: Council of Educational Technology.

Davies, G./ Higgins, J. (1982), *Computers, language and language learning*. London: CILT, Information Guide 22.

Hart, R.S. (1981), "Language study and the PLATO system", *Studies in Language Learning*, 3 (1), pp. 3-6.

Higgins, J./ Johns, T. (1984), *Computers in Language Learning*. London: Collins Educational.

Jung, Udo, ed. (1985), *Man and the Media*. Proceedings of the AILA Symposium at Frankfurt, June 12-15, 1984.

Kenning, M.J./ Kenning, M.-M. (1984), *An Introduction to Computer Assisted Language Teaching*. London: Oxford University Press.

Last, R. W. (1984), *Language Teaching and the Micro*. Oxford: Basil Blackwell.

System, the International Journal of Educational Technology and Language Learning Systems. Oxford: Pergamon Press.

Zettersten, A./ Jacobson, M. (1985), *Brainlearn*. A System for English Language Learning by Microcomputer including authoring programs. Lund: Studentlitteratur AB.

Chapter 4
Viewdata (Videotext).
The use of large databases

Videotex is sometimes used as the covering name for all systems by which textual information is transmitted on a television screen. *Viewdata*, in such a case, is just one variant of videotex. Viewdata like Prestel in Great Britain; (in the Federal Republic of Germany: Bildschirmtext) is an interactive system by which a viewer is connected with a database through his own telephone using a TV monitor, a modem attached to the telephone to convert the incoming signal, and a keyboard. Quite often the word videotext (or interactive videotex) is used instead of viewdata. The French system is called Télématique, the Japanese system is called Captain, and the one used in Hong Kong, Viewdata.

In collaboration with the National Swedish Telecommunications Services and Liber Hermods Publishing House, I developed a vocabulary test system for *Datavision* (Viewdata), in Sweden and Denmark now called *Teledata*, to be used primarily for self-testing. The result for each individual taking the test was a statement indicating the range of his vocabulary. The words were taken from a corpus of c. 10,000 words, thus covering roughly the number of words which a student entering the university is supposed to have mastered. The user proceeds in the viewdata test according to his ability to identify the words indicated on the screen. See fig. 3.

The picture illustrates the lower left part of the tree diagram on which the programming of the vocabulary test is built up.

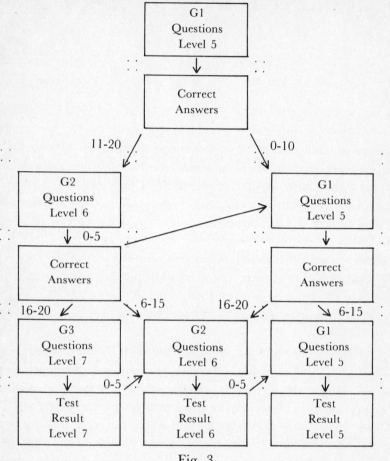

Fig. 3

The words were sub-divided into seven different frequency groups corresponding to the last seven years of the Swedish school system. An example of the words contained in one test picture from Level 7 and the picture showing the correct answers are given below:

1.

1. altitude	2. magnify	3. blackmail
4. nuisance	5. cardboard	6. overwhelmed
7. compatriot	8. pedestrian	9. depressed
10. postpone	11. filth	12. referee
13. gravy	14. spine	15. hedgehog
16. tan	17. incredible	18. tickle
19. laundry	20. valve	

2.
Correct answers to questions 1-20:

1. höjd	2. förstora	3. utpressning
4. besvär	5. papp	6. överväldigad
7. landsman	8. fotgängare	9. deprimerad
10. uppskjuta	11. smuts	12. domare
13. sås	14. ryggrad	15. igelkott
16. solbränna	17. otrolig	18. kittla
19. tvätt	20. ventil	

Approximate answers should also be accepted as correct answers. If you scored 6 or better, press 1. If you scored 0-5, press 2.

Various types of telesoftware, that is, combinations of viewdata and microcomputers, might be mentioned in this context. One example in my own experience is the adapting of some of my microcomputer programs for grammar training to the viewdata system. Although the number of pages that can be transmitted on viewdata is almost unlimited, microcomputers have the advantage of being more interactive, that is, one is not left with the selection of alternatives in a test or exercise but can produce running text of varying length.

A few examples of the type of grammatical items that can be practised with the aid of viewdata will be given below. The examples are taken from a course in LSP.

1. Many businesses today _____ surprised at the many benefits that they might enjoy by using the Rolm MCBX System.

(1) are to be
(2) shall be
(3) would be

(1) Incorrect. The use of this form indicates absolute certainty of a future event.
(2) Incorrect. The use of this form indicates a strong determination or a firm prediction.
(3) Good. Go on to the next question

2. The MCBX system _____ numerous features for the _____ of the
                          (a)   (b)
modern business man.

  a. (1) is offering
     (2) offers
     (3) does offer

  b. (1) convenient
     (2) convenience
     (3) conveniency

  a. (1) Incorrect. This form indicates an event that is limited in time.
     (2) Good. Go on to the next question.
     (3) Incorrect. This form is used for emphasis or affirmation and is not appropriate here.

  b. (1) Incorrect. This is the adjectival form of the word.
     (2) Good. Go on to the next question.
     (3) Incorrect. This form of the word is archaic and no longer in use in Standard English.

3. When you learn about its many features you may wonder if there is
_____ that it cannot do.

(1) anything
(2) nothing
(3) everything

(1) Good. Go on to the next question.

(2) Incorrect. The use of "nothing" with "cannot" forms a double negative that changes the intended meaning of the sentence.

(3) Incorrect. The use of "everything" in this context changes the sentence to mean that it cannot do anything.

4.   The Rolm MCBX System is _____ admired in the international business community.

(1) really
(2) very
(3) very much

(1) Incorrect. This is too imprecise, too informal and slangy.
(2) Incorrect. "Very" cannot be used by itself with the verb "admire".
(3) Good. Go on to the next question.

5.   You may judge its value for yourself when _____ told you about it.

(1) I would have
(2) I have done
(3) I have

(1) Incorrect. This form indicates possibility and lacks the sense of intention that is required here.
(2) Incorrect. This construction does not exist in Standard English.
(3) Good. Go on to the next question.

Some examples of sentences to be used for training grammar (the definite article) on viewdata will also be given:

The definite article
If you think that the definite article should be placed in the blank, press 1 (one). If you think that the article should not be used, press 0 (zero).

1. Richard goes to ...... school at half past seven.

2. I'm going to Paris ...... next week.

3. The sun sets in ...... west.

4. Kate plays ...... piano very well.

5. Do you play ...... tennis?

6. ...... Thames runs through London.

7. Copenhagen is ...... capital of Denmark.

8. Mr and Mrs Davidson get up early in ...... morning.

9. Isn't ...... dinner ready yet?

10. Are you still in ...... bed? It's eight o'clock.

11. In Britain they still keep to ...... left.

12. In Sweden we have kept to ...... right since 1967.

13. The sun rises in ...... east.

14. What's on ...... radio tonight?

15. Tony goes to ...... cinema once a week.

16. I always stay at ...... Grand when I go to Stockholm.

17. ...... Smiths go to the Canaries every year.

18. We generally spend ...... Christmas at home.

19. Tom lives in ...... Oxford Street.

20. Do you think ...... church will be over at twelve?

It is much more difficult to devise exercises concerning content analysis or stylistic training by viewdata. I will suggest one way to practise the appropriate use of passive and active verb forms in the sentences below. Sometimes the difference is quite sophisticated. However, it is possible to train a student's analytic abilities to a certain extent through such an exercise. Again, the examples are part of a course in LSP.

Imagine that you are talking or writing to a customer of your company. Indicate which of the following sentences would be more appropriate

1. (1) I will reply to your letter next week.
   (2) Your letter will be replied to next week.

   (1) Good. Go on to the next question.
   (2) Not the best alternative. The passive form of the verb makes the sentence sound cold and impersonal.

2. (1) We regret that production costs have risen and that we must pass our increased expenses on to the customer.
   (2) It is regrettable that production costs have risen and that increased expenses must be passed on to the customer.

   (1) Not the best alternative. In the case of such bad news the active form of the verb helps to make the process sound too obviously a matter of personal choice.
   (2) Good. Go on to the next question.

3. (1) Our records indicate that you have lapsed in your payments to us.
   (2) Our records indicate that your payments to us have lapsed.

   (1) Not the best alternative. The directness of the active form of the verb seems insulting and accusatory to the recipient. The passive form would make the sentence less personal, therefore more polite in this instance.
   (2) Good. Go on to the next question.

4. (1) The names of the customers he meets are always remembered by the sales manager.
   (2) The sales manager always remembers the names of the customers he meets.

   (1) Not the best alternative. The passive form of the verb makes the sentence awkward-sounding and unnecessarily long.
   (2) Good. Go on to the next question.

5. (1) Among those who use it, a highly favourable impression has been created by our product.
   (2) Our product has created a highly favourable impression among those who use it.

   (1) Not the best alternative. Lacking in emphasis, strength and force. The passive form of the verb dissipates the strength of the sentence.
   (2) Good. Go on to the next question.

6. (1) We regret to say that the deadline for delivery of replacement parts will not be met.
   (2) We regret to say that we cannot meet the deadline for delivery of replacement parts.

(1) Good. Go on to the next question.

(2) Not the best alternative. The active form of the verb emphasizes that the fault is ours. The passive form of the verb would work toward mitigating the negative content of the sentence by impersonalizing it.

7. (1) We are pleased that a reduction in price for our 1984 models can be offered.

   (2) We are pleased that we can offer a reduction in price for our 1984 models.

   (1) Not the best alternative. The passive form of the verb weakens and dispels the directness and force that such an announcement deserves.

   (2) Good. Go on to the next question.

8. (1) We assume that you are still interested in increased efficiency in your business so we are taking the liberty of sending you our latest brochure on the subject.

   (2) It is assumed that you are still interested in increased efficiency in your business so the liberty has been taken of sending you our latest brochure on the subject.

   (1) Good. Go on to the next question.

   (1) Not the best alternative. The passive form of the verbs in this sentence contributes toward a lack of direct personal contact and a sense of vagueness.

9. (1) Export must be relied on by manufacturers in Europe and Japan to make their investments pay, while their home markets are defended against foreign competition.

   (2) Manufacturers in Europe and Japan must rely on export to make their investments pay, while defending their home markets against foreign competition.

   (1) Not the best alternative. The passive form of the verbs makes the information of the sentence diffuse and uncertain.

   (2) Good. Go on to the next question.

10. (1) We hope that you have by now received the shipment about which you enquired in your recent letter.

(2) It is hoped that by now the shipment about which you enquired in your recent letter has been received.

(1) Good. That completes this section. Please go on to the next section.
(2) Not the best alternative. The passive form of the verb creates a tone that is stiff, formal and impersonal.

So far viewdata has usually been discussed in such contexts as home banking and teleshopping, but the potential of viewdata in education is great. This is particularly true since the advantage of gaining access to large databases, word banks, dictionaries, encyclopedias, information systems, etc. is so great.

The extension of a viewdata system to a database, thus connecting two different systems, is usually called a *gateway*. In Britain, for example, the *Prestel Gateway* makes it possible for Prestel users to gain access to various databases. In Denmark, Gyldendal's *Encyclopedia* is an example of the use of encyclopedic databases in education. See figure 4: Gyldendal's *Encyclopedia*. In the Federal Republic of Germany there is, for example, *Meyers Bildschirmlexikon*.

The access to large databases will certainly open up new possibilities both for home-users, schools and also for larger organizations. Such databases on mainframe computers can, for example, be reached through a telephone link. With the aid of a microcomputer and the telephone system it is possible to get access to databases, for example, EUDISED, which is a European coverage of educational research projects.

The advantages of the access to some of the large databases include the ability to examine the contexts of the words in which you are interested. Examples of contextualized CAL programs can be found in J. Fox, "Computer-assisted vocabulary learning", *ELT Journal,* vol. 38 (1984), pp. 27-33. This means that one may easily devise tests or exercises in LSP, for example technical English, where the context used is authentic, that is, taken directly from the specific database.

Fig. 4. Extracts from the *Encyclopedia* and the corresponding database.

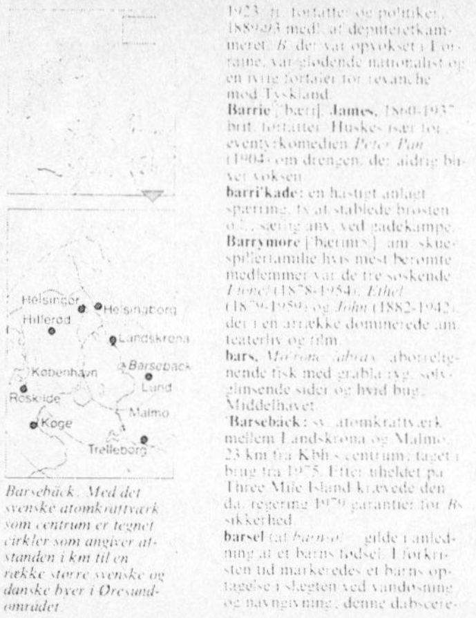

o.l.; særlig anv. ved gadekampe.
Barrymore ['bærimɔ:]: am. skue-
spillerfamilie hvis mest berømte
medlemmer var de tre søskende
Lionel (1878-1954), *Ethel*
(1879-1959) og *John* (1882-1942),
der i en årrække dominerede am.
teaterliv og film.
bars, *Mo'rone 'labrax:* aborrelig-
nende fisk med gråblå ryg, sølv-
glinsende sider og hvid bug;
Middelhavet.
'Barsebäck: sv. atomkraftværk
mellem Landskrona og Malmö,
23 km fra Kbh.s centrum; taget i
brug fra 1975. Efter uheldet på
Three Mile Island krævede den
da. regering 1979 garantier for *B*s
sikkerhed.
barsel (af *barnsøl)*: gilde i anled-

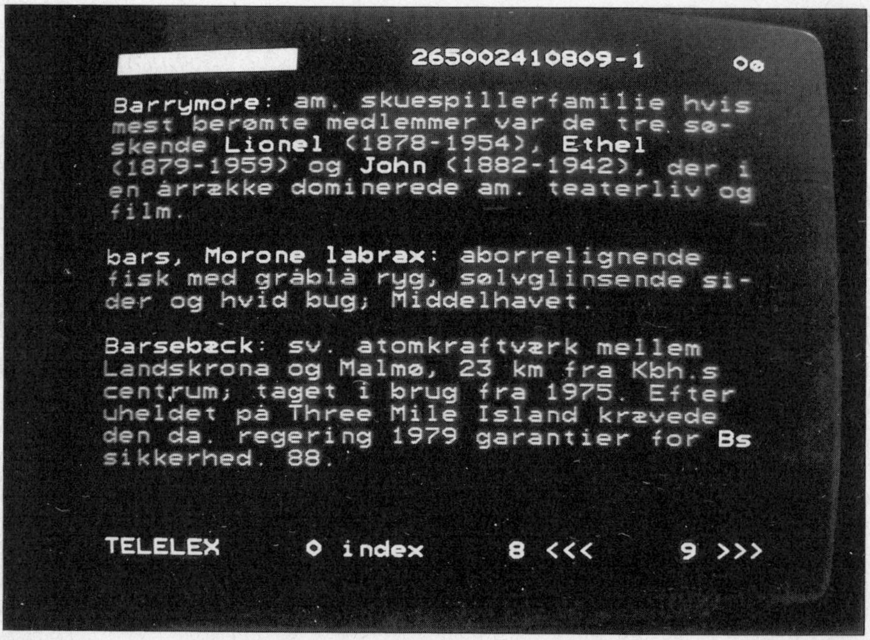

Figure 5 shows the contents of the Brown University Corpus, containing circa 1 million words of running text, fig. 6 all the texts
contained in category J (Scientific English), and fig. 7, the rank order
of the 50 most frequent words in category J. Fig. 8, finally, shows the
corresponding rank order in Category A (Press: Reportage).

Fig. 5. The Brown University Corpus.

I. *Informative Prose:* 374 samples

  A. Press: Reportage

Political	Daily: 10	Weekly: 4	Total: 14
Sports	- 5	- 2	- 7
Society	- 3	- 0	- 3
Spot News	- 7	- 2	- 9
Financial	- 3	- 1	- 4
Cultural	- 5	- 2	- <u>7</u>
			= 44

  B. Press: Editorial

Institutional	Daily: 7	Weekly: 3	Total: 10
Personal	- 7	- 3	- 10
Letters to the Editor	- 5	- 2	- <u>7</u>
			= 27

  C. Press: Reviews (theatre, books, music, dance) .... Daily: 14 Weekly: 3 Total: <u>17</u>
                                                           = 17

  D. Religion

Books	7
Periodicals	6
Tracts	<u>4</u>
	= 17

  E. Skills and Hobbies

Books	2
Periodicals	<u>34</u>
	= 36

  F. Popular Lore

Books	23
Periodicals	<u>25</u>
	= 48

  G. Belles Lettres, Biography, Memoirs, etc.

Books	38
Periodicals	<u>37</u>
	= 75

Fig. 6. The texts of the corpus (category J)

01	Cornell H. Mayer	Radio Emission of the Moon and Planets
02	R.C. Binder et al.	1961 Heat Transfer & Fluid Mechanics Institute
03	Harry H. Hull	Normal Forces & Their Thermodynamic Significance
04	James a. Ibers et al.	Proton Magnetic Resonance Study
05	John R. Van Wazer, ed.	Phosphorus and Its Compounds
06	Francis J. Johnston & John E. Willard	Exchange Reaction Between Cl_2 and CCl_4
07	J.F. Vedder	Micrometeorites
08	Le Roy Fothergill	Biological Warfare
09	M. Yokoyama el al.	Chemical & Serological Characteristics
10	B.J.D. Meeuse	The Story of Pollination
11	Clifford H. Pope	The Giant Snakes
12	Richard F. McLaughlin et al.	A Study of the Subgross Pulmonary Anatomy
13	S. Idell Pyle et al.	Onsets, Completions & Spans
14	Jacob Robbins et al.	The Thyroid-Stimulating Hormone
15	J.W.C. Hagstrom et al.	Debilitating Muscular Weakness
16	A.N. Nagaraj & L.M. Black	Localization of Wound-Tumor Virus Antigen
17	E. Gellhorn	Prolegomena to a Theory of the Emotions
18	Kenneth Hoffman & Ray Kunze	Linear Algebra
19	Frederick Mosteller et al.	Probability with Statistical Applications
20	R.P. Jerrard	Inscribed Squares in Plane Curves
21	C.R. Wylie, Jr.	Line Involutions in S3
22	Max F. Millikan & Donald L. Blackmer, editors	The Emerging Nations
23	Joyce O. Hertzler	American Social Institutions

Fig. 7. Rank order (Category J)

Word – Frequency list

rank	frequency	relative frequency	word form
1	12536	0,079263	THE
2	7454	0,047130	OF
3	4282	0,027074	AND
4	4097	0,025904	IN
5	3948	0,024962	TO
6	3467	0,021921	A
7	2409	0,015232	IS
8	1711	0,010818	THAT
9	1568	0,009914	FOR
10	1361	0,008605	BE
11	1291	0,008163	AS
12	1216	0,007689	BY
13	1158	0,007322	WITH
14	1146	0,007246	IT
15	1115	0,007050	WAS
16	993	0,006279	THIS
17	993	0,006279	ARE
18	954	0,006032	ON
19	905	0,005722	OR
20	835	0,005280	WHICH
21	792	0,005008	FROM
22	783	0,004951	NOT
23	739	0,004673	AN
24	739	0,004673	AT
25	634	0,004009	WERE
26	551	0,003484	HAVE
27	526	0,003326	WE
28	521	0,003294	ONE
29	501	0,003168	BUT
30	454	0,002871	HIS
31	431	0,002725	HAS
32	421	0,002662	THESE
33	412	0,002605	THERE
34	409	0,002586	BEEN
35	405	0,002561	THEY
36	395	0,002498	MORE
37	388	0,002453	HE
38	369	0,002333	THEIR
39	367	0,002320	CAN

40	362	0,002289	ALL
41	339	0,002143	WILL
42	336	0,002124	ONLY
43	334	0,002112	MAY
44	334	0,002112	THAN
45	332	0,002099	IF
46	331	0,002093	HAD
47	321	0,002030	WOULD
48	316	0,001998	SUCH
49	312	0,001973	WHEN
50	311	0,001966	SOME

Fig. 8. Rank order (Category A)

Word – Frequency list

rank	frequency	relative frequency	word form
1	6385	0,073633	THE
2	2858	0,032959	OF
3	2185	0,025198	AND
4	2162	0,024933	A
5	2143	0,024713	TO
6	2020	0,023295	IN
7	969	0,011175	FOR
8	829	0,009560	THAT
9	733	0,008453	IS
10	717	0,008269	WAS
11	691	0,007969	ON
12	642	0,007404	HE
13	637	0,007346	AT
14	567	0,006539	WITH
15	526	0,006066	BE
16	520	0,005997	AS
17	504	0,005812	BY
18	478	0,005512	IT
19	428	0,004936	HIS
20	406	0,004682	SAID
21	389	0,004486	WILL
22	353	0,004071	FROM
23	330	0,003806	ARE

24	320	0,003690	THIS
25	311	0,003587	AN
26	301	0,003471	HAS
27	283	0,003264	BUT
28	281	0,003241	HAD
29	268	0,003091	THEY
30	268	0,003091	WHO
31	265	0,003056	HAVE
32	259	0,002987	WERE
33	257	0,002964	NOT
34	254	0,002929	MRS
35	246	0,002837	WOULD
36	245	0,002825	WHICH
37	241	0,002779	NEW
38	231	0,002664	THEIR
39	213	0,002456	ONE
40	212	0,002445	BEEN
41	203	0,002341	ITS
42	188	0,002168	THERE
43	185	0,002133	I
44	184	0,002122	MORE
45	181	0,002087	ALL
46	177	0,002041	LAST
47	176	0,002030	OR
48	174	0,002007	TWO
49	170	0,001960	MR
50	169	0,001949	WHEN

The term *telesoftware* is used for the transmission of programs from one computer to another. Telesoftware can be broadcast via a teletext system or transmitted by telephone via viewdata. Using a viewdata system, for example one such as Prestel in Britain, computer programs can be introduced on the TV screen and then "downloaded" to a microcomputer.

It is easy to see that telesoftware as described above may have a bearing on the development of systems for distance education. This will be discussed further in Chapter 12.

Dictionaries, existing in machine-readable form, such as the *Longman Dictionary of Contemporary English* and the *Collins English Dictionary*, are examples of lexical databases. On linquistic databases, see further G. Leech-A. Beale, "Computers in English Language Research",

Language Teaching: The International Abstracting Journal for Language Teachers and Applied Linguistics, Vol. 17:3 (1984), pp. 216-29, and M. van Halteren, "User interface for a linguistic data base", *ICAME News*, 8:1 (1984), pp. 31-40.

Chapter 4: **Sources and further reading**

D'Antoni, S.G. (1982), "Videodisc and Videotex: New Media for distance Education", in J.S. Daniel, *et.al.*, *Learning at a Distance*, pp. 287-90.

Fedida, S./ Malik, R. (1979), *The Viewdata Revolution*. London: Associated Business Programmers Ltd.

Förster, Hans-Peter (1983), *Bildschirmtext*. München: Humboldt-Taschenbuchverlag.

Gateway. CET Information Sheet No. 10 (1984). London: Council for Educational Technology.

Hurly, P. (1982), "Using Videotex in Distance Education", in J.S. Daniel, *et al.*, *Learning at a Distance*, p. 109.

Kühlwein, W./ Raasch, A., eds. (1984), *Bildschirmtext. Perspektiven eines neuen Mediums*. Tübingen: Gunter Narr Verlag.

Madden, J. (1979). *Videotex in Canada*. Ottawa: Ministry of Supply and Services.

Martin, J. (1982), *Viewdata and the Information Society*. Hemel Hempstead: Prentice Hall International.

Sigel, E., ed. (1980), *Videotext: The Coming Revolution in Home/Office Information Retrieval*. White Plains, New York: Knowledge Industry Publications, Inc.

Telesoftware. CET Information Sheet No. 3 (November 1982). London: Council for Educational Technology.

Thompson, V. (1982), *Prestel and Education: a report of a one year trial*. London: Council for Educational Technology.

Thompson, V. *et al.* (1982), *Videotex in Education: a new technology briefing*. London: Council for Educational Technology.

Tydeman, J. *et al.* (1982), *Teletext and Videotext in the United States: Market, Potential, Technology*. New York: McGraw-Hill.

Videotex Systems. USPEC 32 d (March 1984). London: Council for Educational Technology.

Chapter 5
Teletext. Teleflashes

Teletext is a non-interactive system, whereby unused lines of television signal can carry textual material such as news, airline schedules, classified ads, etc. In Britain the teletext systems are called Ceefax (BBC) and Oracle (ITV); in France Antiope; and in Canada Telidon. In collaboration with Utbildningsradion at the Swedish Broadcasting Corporation, I created a system whereby vocabulary can be reinforced before, during and after language programmes or documentary programmes on TV. By using the teletext technique, by superimposing text on the documentary, certain crucial phrases in, for example, "Panorama of the Week" could be explained. These explanations, which I called teleflashes, were subdivided into three levels of difficulty, and the viewer could select the level corresponding to his own competence. There was a teletext introduction before the programme, and several tests after the programme, reinforcing the words and phrases learned and providing some comprehension exercises. It is possible to call up the teletext pages one needs either before, during or after the TV programme. The whole idea was to provide educational and other programmes with a technique whereby English could be learned by viewers without textbooks or the ordinary subtitles in Swedish.

An extract from the beginning of a programme in the series "Panorama of the Week" is given below (with teleflashes in the margin):

Robert Mugabe has praised Sweden for *providing* humanitarian aid to the black national struggle for *independence* and for continuing aid after his government came to power. Sweden so far has been providing support as catastrophe assistance. Now the visiting prime minister and Swedish prime minister Torbjörn Fälldin have signed the first regular *foreign aid agreement* between the two countries making Zimbabwe one of the regular receiving nations of Swedish foreign aid. The program provides some 20 million dollars for the budget year ending next July. About a fifth of the aid is to be used to buy products and *counselling* service in Sweden. The Swedes indicate that they may increase the percentage of *tied aid* in the future as well. A third of the money is to be used for the rehabilitation of the many refugees in Zimbabwe and the remaining half is to be used to improve health care education and the nation's infrastructure. Bill Schiller with that report.

In order to explain how the whole learning process was built up, the teletext introduction with the key-words given for each part of "Panorama of the Week" will be reproduced in English.

PANORAMA OF THE WEEK (on teletext)

Picture 1

In Panorama of the Week this time all of the most important and difficult words and expressions will be explained at the bottom of the picture.

Before the programme, some of the key-words in the text will be introduced and explained.

Picture 2

After the programme you are invited to test yourself. You may test whether you have understood the most important words and expressions. You may also test whether you have understood the contents of certain parts of the programme correctly.

Picture 3

Contents of the TV-programme

1. Introduction
2. Robert Mugabe
3. The L.O. Congress
4. Conversation lessons in commuter trains.
5. The Swedish Foreign Minister, Mr Ola Ullsten, addresses the General Assembly of the United Nations.
6. Research report on the Lapp culture.
7. New contract for Kockum's Shipyard.
8. The new translation of the New Testament.

Picture 4

Introduction to the first part of Panorama

The Prime Minister of Zimbabwe, Mr Robert Mugabe, has been on an official visit to Sweden.

The new African state Zimbabwe, earlier called Rhodesia, received black majority rule in 1980.

Picture 5

Map of Zimbabwe

Picture 6

Key-words:

The following words and expressions are essential for the understanding of the various parts of Panorama of the Week.

Part II: Robert Mugabe in Sweden

the elections = allmänna val
civil war = inbördeskrig
government = regering
independence = självstyre, oberoende
foreign aid agreement = biståndsavtal
tied aid = bundet bistånd
refugee = flykting

Picture 7

Part III: The L.O. Congress

trade union = fackförening
agenda = föredragningslista, dagordning
Board of Directors = styrelse, direktion
co-determination law = medbestämmandelag
the rank and file = de djupa leden
unemployment = arbetslöshet
relief programmes = beredskapsarbete
wage-earner funds, employee investment funds = löntagarfonder
payroll = lönelista, löner
employee = anställd, löntagare

Picture 8

Part IV: Conversation lessons in commuter trains

commuter train = pendeltåg
adult education = vuxenutbildning
colloquial English = talspråksengelska
crossword puzzle = korsord

Picture 9

Part V: Ola Ullsten addressing the General Assembly

General Assembly = Generalförsamling
nuclear arsenal = kärnvapenarsenal
negotiating table = förhandlingsbord
nuclear-free zone = kärnvapenfri zon
human rights = mänskliga rättigheter

Picture 10

Part VI: Research report on the Lapp culture

reindeer = ren
urban environment = stadsmiljö
brand = märka
dental assistant = tandsköterska

Picture 11

Part VII: New contract for Kockum's shipyard

shipyard = varv
tender = anbud, offert
roll-on-roll-off vessel = ro-ro-fartyg
negotiation = förhandling
rolling mill = valsverk
redundancy = arbetslöshet, friställande

Picture 12

Part VIII:The new translation of the New Testament

publishing house = bokförlag
state appointed bible commission = statlig bibelkommission
colloquialism = talspråk
transmission = utsändning.

Picture 13

If you wish full subtitles in "Panorama of the Week" press**.
    If your prefer to reinforce words and phrases through teleflashes, this can be done on three different levels.

1. If your vocabulary is excellent, press 1 and only the most difficult words will be given in teleflashes.

Picture 14

2. If your vocabulary is less advanced, press 2 and some of the less difficult words will also be explained.
3. If you regard your vocabulary as normal, press 3, and most of the important words will appear in teleflashes.

    If you want a brief diagnostic test, press 4.

After the TV-programme, a series of tests were offered on teletext. They tested vocabulary as well as comprehension. Three pictures from the multiple choice vocabulary test will be given below.

VOCABULARY TEST

Picture 1

1. DAMAGES (A) farligheter (B) skadestånd (C) besvär
2. DESTINY (A) öde (B) motstånd (C) mål
3. INDEPENDENCE (A) beroende (B) självstyre (C) jubileum
4. REFUGEE (A) undanflykt (B) räddning (C) flykting
5. TIED AID (A) bundet bistånd (B) koppling (C) flykting
6. TRADE UNION (A) försöksverksamhet (B) fackförening
   (C) handelsavtal
7. BOARD OF DIRECTORS (A) förhandlingsbord (B) direktion
   (C) direktionsassistent
8. WAGE EARNER (A) löntagare (B) arbetsgivare (C) lånekamrer

Press R and you will get the correct answers.

Picture 2

1. EMPLOYEE (A) arbetsgivare (B) anställning (C) anställd
2. ADULT EDUCATION (A) vuxenutbildning (B) barnprogram
   (C) distansundervisning
3. TOPICAL SUBJECTS (A) vanliga medborgare (B) aktuella ämnen
   (C) farliga beståndsdelar
4. NEGOTIATE (A) förhala (B) förhandla (C) försvåra
5. INTERFERE (A) blanda sig i (B) skjuta ifrån sig (C) förhandla
6. ALLEVIATE (A) försvåra (B) famla (C) lindra.
7. ENVIRONMENT (A) svårighet (B) miljö (C) avtal
8. NEGOTIATE (A) förneka (B) förhandla (C) minska

Press R and you will get the correct answers.

Picture 3

1. CO-DETERMINATION (A) motsträvighet (B) ordergiving
   (C) medbestämmande
2. RANK AND FILE (A) de djupa leden (B) hit och dit
   (C) överbefälet
3. RELIEF PROGRAMME (A) nödhjälpsarbete (B) smärtlindring
   (C) arbetsmarknad
4. COMMUTER TRAIN (A) elektriskt lok (B) pendeltåg (C) rälsbuss

5. HUMAN RIGHTS (A)arbetsrätt (B) människoföda
   (C) mänskliga rättigheter
6. DENTAL ASSISTANT (A) nödhjälp (B) tandsköterska
   (C) sjuksköterska
7. ROLLING MILL (A) kaffekvarn (B) rullskridskobana (C) valsverk
8. PUBLISHING HOUSE (A) krog (B) agentur (C) förlag

Press R and you will get the correct answers

I shall also give another example of an experiment with teleflashes. In the second experiment the BBC series, "The Living City", was used. The second programme in this series, "A Family Affair," was selected as the one to be used for this experiment. The beginning of the programme contained some difficult vocabulary and required several explanations in the form of teleflashes, perhaps too many for the eye to catch.

The introduction with teleflashes runs as follows:

The family is a *crucial unit* in our society. It's
one of the *prime agents* shaping our *destinies*. As
children and *adolescents* we're *moulded* by family
life and this has a strong influence on our
educational chances and choice of career
amongst other things. As *adults,* we look to the
family for *companionship,* emotional security
and sexual activity. In old age we look to it for
comfort and support. 70 % of the British adult
population is married and 75 % of *divorced*
people remarry. The family is a very popular
institution.

central enhet		
de starkaste krafterna	öde
ungdom	forma	

| vuxen |
| sällskap |

| tröst |
| skild |

The words and phrases were sub-divided into three levels in the following manner:

Level 1	crucial unit	adolescent
	the prime agents	mould

Level 2	destiny
	adult
	companionship

Level 3	comfort
	divorced

Before the programme the following pictures were shown to the viewers on teletext:

Picture 1

This programme gives you a picture of life in three different types of families. The three main types of families that are shown:

1. *The nuclear family:* a family consisting of man, wife and one or more children.
2. *The extended family:* a family including a number of close relatives.
3. *The one-parent family:* consisting of a mother or father and one or more children.

Picture 2

The following variants of English can be observed in the programme:

1. Colloquial English, for example, the use of "me arm" instead of "my arm."
2. Dialect features from the local dialect of Leicester.
3. A variant of African-Asiatic English spoken by the family from Uganda.
4. A special sociological terminology, for example such terms as "conjugal roles" (=äktenskapliga roller).

After the programme was shown, both a comprehension test and a vocabulary test were given.

The following questions are taken from the comprehension test:

Picture 1

Which of the following statements is true?

1. 90 % of divorced people in Britain remarry.

2. 75 % of divorced people in Britain remarry.

3. 16 % of divorced people in Britain remarry.

4. 35 % of divorced people in Britain remarry.

Picture 2

The Trewernes family, consisting of man, wife and three children, can be called

1. An extended family
2. A nuclear family
3. A one-parent family

Picture 3

The average family in Victorian England had about

1. Twelve children
2. Four children
3. Six children
4. One child

Picture 4

Research shows that the greater part of housework and child-minding is done by

1. the man
2. man and woman together
3. the woman

Picture 5

At the beginning of this century, the mean age for women in England was

1. c. 30 years of age.
2. c. 45 years of age.
3. c. 52 years of age.
4. c. 65 years of age.

An example of the multiple choice vocabulary test from each level will also be given. The first example is a test of words belonging to level 3. The correct answer is underlined.

1. SOCIETY (A) socialism (B) <u>samhälle</u> (C) kunskap
2. CHOICE (A) <u>val</u> (B) välja (C) lust
3. DIVORCED (A) diverse (B) <u>skild</u> (C) varierad
4. PATTERN (A) makt (B) tillgång (C) <u>mönster</u>
5. INFANT (A) <u>spädbarn</u> (B) snabb (C) vuxen
6. MORTALITY (A) födsel (B) <u>dödlighet</u> (C) avdrag
7. CONSEQUENTLY (A) antagligen (B) nästan (C) <u>följaktligen</u>
8. NIECE (A) trevlig (B) <u>brorsdotter</u> (C) morbror
9. CONSCIOUS (A) vanlig (B) konstig (C) <u>medveten</u>
10. TAX (A) böter (B) <u>skatt</u> (C) inkomst

The second example represents level 2.

1. DESTINY (A) öde (B) fördel (C) förakt
2. ADULT (A) varsam (B) vuxen (C) minderårig
3. DELIBERATE (A) skadlig (B) frivillig (C) avsiktlig
4. CASUAL (A) tillfällig (B) våldsam (C) betydande

5. EXTENDED (A) minskad (B) utökad (C) befriad
6. AUTHORITY (A) villkor (B) skada (C) myndighet
7. CRADLE (A) slev (B) vagga (C) etikett
8. REASSURANCE (A) lugn (B) återverkan (C) klarhet
9. BRASS (A) koppar (B) mörker (C) mässing
10. CONTEMPORARY (A) tydlig (B) samtida (C) tillfällig

The third example represents level 1.

1. ADOLESCENT (A) skimmer (B) ungdom (C) blomstrande
2. MOULD (A) slipa (B) krossa (C) forma
3. CONSECRATED (A) firad (B) helgad (C) bränd
4. VASECTOMY (A) övervikt (B) alstring (C) sterilisering
5. NUCLEAR FAMILY (A) kärnfamilj (B) storfamilj (C) barnfamilj
6. PROXIMITY (A) närhet (B) avstånd (C) hastighet
7. EQUIVALENT (A) bundenhet (B) knutpunkt (C) motsvarighet
8. STIGMA (A) brännmärkning (B) gåta (C) försörjning
9. MATRIMONY (A) mödravård (B) äktenskap (C) motstånd
10. CONJUGAL (A) äktenskaplig (B) barnslig (C) oäkta

One difference between the first experiment ("Panorama of the Week") and the second ("The Living City") was that "The Living City" was used as a course in English on Swedish Television. Therefore a textbook with introductions and word-lists was written (by David Wright) for the course. A student having access to both the textbook, the teletext exercises, and to the teleflashes during the programme would certainly get the utmost from a series of this nature.

In the case of "Panorama of the Week", which was broadcast as a regular weekly programme, it would sometimes be difficult to have sufficient teletext pages available for the purpose of defining the difficult words and phrases in the text, and it was also difficult to find sufficient time to produce the number of pages required.

For introducing radio and TV-programmes, for providing glossaries, teleflashes, tests and exercises, teletext is undoubtedly a most useful technique, as the two experiments above clearly demonstrated. The use of teletext for distance education and for self-education will be further discussed in Chapter 12.

Chapter 5: **Sources and further reading**

Nilsson, J. (1983), *Integrerad text-TV i utbildningsradio*. Stockholm: Sveriges utbild-ningsradio.

Sigel, E., ed. (1980), *Videotext: The Coming Revolution in Home/Office Information Retrieval*. White Plains, New York: Knowledge Industry Publications, Inc.

Thompson, V. *et al.* (1982), *Videotex in Education: a new technology briefing*. London: Council for Educational Technology.

Tydeman, J. *et al.* (1982), *Teletext and Videotext in the United States: Market, Potential, Technology*. New York: McGraw-Hill.

Veith, R. H. (1983), *Television's Teletext*. New York: North-Holland.

Videotex Systems. *USPEC* 32 d (March 1984). London: Council for Educational Tech-nology.

Zettersten, A. (1985), "Language training and testing by means of new electronic media", in Jung, U. (ed.), *Man and the Media*.

Chapter 6

Making your own video programme.
The functional approach.
Videodiscs

The video boom started even earlier than the microcomputer revolution. As in the case of microcomputers, authors and publishers were somewhat reluctant in the beginning to use video in language training. Language teachers had primarily used video programmes in the 1970's as authentic illustrations of life-like situations. Very little additional training material was used in conjunction with such documentary video films.

The functional/notional approach to language learning, as described in Chapter 2, has been used in some TV productions which are available on video.

The technique for language learning with the aid of video, which I am going to describe here, has not, however, previously been explored to any significant extent in Europe.

The experiments with *video* production were made in the TV studio at the University of Copenhagen. The idea was to practise language functions in a new way during oral proficiency classes in the English Department. The students were given a general topic area – in this case, "Business in Hong Kong", and a set of *language functions* which they were asked to concentrate on while making the video programme. The following language functions, according to the specifications of functions found in van Ek (1976) were given:

I. *Imparting and seeking factual information*
    1. Identifying
    2. Asking

II. *Expressing and finding out intellectual attitudes*
1. Expressing agreement and disagreement
2. Accepting an order or invitation
3. Inquiring whether something is considered possible or impossible

III. *Expressing and finding out emotional attitudes*
1. Expressing pleasure, liking
2. Expressing displeasure, dislike
3. Expressing interest or lack of interest
4. Expressing surprise
5. Expressing gratitude
6. Expressing intention
7. Expressing want, desire

IV. *Expressing and finding out moral attitudes*
1. Expressing approval
2. Expressing disapproval
3. Expressing appreciation

V. *Getting things done*
1. Suggesting a course of action
2. Requesting others to do something
3. Instructing or directing others to do something

VI. *Socializing*
1. Greeting people
2. Introducing people
3. Taking leave
4. Proposing a toast
5. Making an appointment
6. Invitation to a party

The following specific actions (cf. van Ek) were also given:

1. Personal identification
2. Profession or occupation
3. Accommodation

4. Entertainment
5. Travel
6. Public transport
7. Entering and leaving a country
8. Invitations
9. Shopping
10. Clothes, fashion
11. Food and drink
12. Eating and drinking out
13. Telephone
14. Places
15. Weather

The students were asked to write a brief synopsis, and at our next meeting to improvise on the basis of the synopsis – using most of the language functions already given.

Since there is so little documentation of similar experiments based on a functional/notional approach, the result must be regarded as quite unique at this level. Some schools have now started similar experiments both in Denmark and in Sweden but there is no material as yet in published form.

The following scenes were given and the synopsis was written on the basis of the following eight scenes:

Scenes
1. Telephone contact.
   Hansen Quality Shirts, Denmark, and
   Chinese Quality Clothing Inc., Hong Kong.
2. Meeting in Danish office.
3. Telephone contact. Planning a trip to Hong Kong.
4. Airport scene. Hong Kong.
5. Night club. Hong Kong.
6. Morning after the night-club. Hong Kong. Meeting. Samples discussed.
7. Meeting with Chinese representative. Hong Kong.
8. Signing the contract. Hong Kong.

During the writing of the synopsis and the rehearsals of all the scenes, the students used the target language with the specific aim of producing a good video film. The language instruction by the teacher was carried out with a very light hand. In fact, I was one of the team in the production of the film and the ordinary teaching situation was transcended and replaced with genuine interaction. The students certainly lost the characteristic inhibitions of non-native speakers and communication proceeded in a natural and relaxed manner.

As a learning experience the planning and performing of "Business in Hong Kong" yielded three important results:

1. How to make a video film.
2. Communication in English based on a functional/notional approach.
3. Business English.

In order to illustrate how language functions were practised, a short extract from the beginning of Scene 4, Airport Scene, Hong Kong, will be provided below.

Scene 4:
Hong Kong Airport

Harald Jørgensen: I wonder where Mr Wang Si Lai is. He promised to meet us here at the airport.

Miss Hansen Junior: Yes, but where?

Avant Garde: Oh, he'll turn up alright. Don't worry.

Miss Hansen Junior: Probably.

Wang Si Lai: Excuse me but are you the representatives from Hansen Quality Shirts, Denmark?

Harald Jørgensen: Yes, we certainly are. Then you must be Mr Wang Si Lai.

Wang Si Lai: Yes, I am.

Harald Jørgensen: I'm Harald Jørgensen, pleased to meet you.

Wang Si Lai: Hello, Mr Jørgensen, nice to meet you.

Harald Jørgensen: May I introduce ... This is our manager, Miss Hansen Junior.

Miss Hansen Junior: How do you do?

Wang Si Lai: Hello, Miss Hansen Junior, nice to meet you.

Miss Hansen Junior: Nice of you to be here.

Harald Jørgensen: And this is our famous French designer, Mr Avant Garde.

Wang Si Lai: Hello, Mr Avant Garde.

Avant Garde: Pleased to meet you.

Wang Si Lai: I've heard so much about you.

Avant Garde: Thank you very much.

Wang Si Lai: Well, did you all have a good flight?

All together: Yes, we did. Very nice, indeed.

Wang Si Lai: You see, I have booked rooms for you at the Mandarin. And I have arranged a tour to a very famous nightclub called "Harbour View". I hope you will enjoy that.

Avant Garde: I've heard about that.

Harald Jørgensen: Certainly.

Wang Si Lai: Good. Will you all please follow me outside? My chauffeur is waiting. And don't worry about your luggage, I'll send for that.

Harald Jørgensen: Oh, very good.

Wang Si Lai: This way please.

Harald Jørgensen: Thank you very much.

After the video film had been recorded, we analysed it scene by scene and discussed all of the functions practised, together with all of the errors of grammar, pronunciation and intonation. There was a good deal of feedback and, thus, an additional, fourth result of the learning experience should be added to the foregoing list: Language Pedagogy.

All language functions were listed in a kind of protocol with space left for commentary as we proceeded to criticize the various scenes afterwards. The airport scene recorded above dealt chiefly with functions like greeting people, introducing people, expressing intention, gratitude, etc. The various functions of a telephone conversation will be described in chapter 10, dealing specifically with the use of the telephone in language learning. In this context the functions of two scenes will be listed, merely to show the methods used to analyse our results and to obtain maximum feedback.

The functions of scene 2 below illustrate a meeting in a Danish office, while those of scene 5 illustrate a visit to a Hong Kong nightclub.

EARLY 196-220	I.1 I.2 III.3 V.1 VI.1	Identifying Asking Expressing interest or lack of interest Suggesting a course of action Greeting people
MIDDLE 221-240	I.1 I.2 II.1 V.1	Identifying Asking Expressing agreement and disageement Suggesting a course of action
LATE 241-268	I.1 I.2 II.3 III.7 IV.1 IV.2 IV.3 V.I VI.3	Identifying Asking Inquiring whether something is possible or impossible Expressing want, desire Expressing approval Expressing disapproval Expressing appreciation Suggesting a course of action Taking leave

EARLY 339-350	I.1	Identifying
	I.2	Asking
	II.2	Accepting an offer or invitation
	III.1	Expressing pleasure
	III.3	Expressing interest or lack of interest
	III.7	Expressing want, desire
	VI.1	Greeting people
	VI.2	Introducing people
MIDDLE 351-370 (mainly music)	II.1	Expressing agreement and disagreement
	III.7	Expressing want, desire
LATE 371-390	I.1	Identifying
	I.2	Asking
	III.1	Expressing pleasure, liking
	VI.4	Proposing a toast

When analysing the students' communicative competence during the course of the semester in which we worked together, I used the standard diagnostic test sheet developed by the English Department of the University of Copenhagen. A sample test sheet appears below:

Diagnostic test advice sheet   *Name:* _____

A. LISTENING   You scored _____ out of 18, which indicates that your listening comprehension is good / fair / poor.

B. READING   You need to pay attention to:

weak forms: reduced vowels in articles, prepositions, etc.

intonation: melody, rhythm, emphasis

word stress: main stress on _____

reduced vowels in _____

problem words: pronunciation of _____

C. COMPOSITION   You need to concentrate on:

fluency: building sentences into more complex, larger units

accuracy: using grammar and vocabulary correctly

variety: extending your range of usage and idiom

intelligibility: using intonation with more expressiveness

pronunciation: keeping to standard British/American

speed: talking with ease and confidence.

D. WORD-SOUND RELATIONS   You scored _____ out of 14, which is good / fair / poor.

PROBLEM SOUNDS   Symbols from N. Davidsen-Nielsen, *Engelsk Fonetik*.

NB This list is selective, not comprehensive.

	consonants				vowels
	initial	medial	final	/iː/	heed
/p,b/		happy	rib	/ɪ/	hid
/t/	ten	matter	light	/æ/	had
/d/		muddle	lied	/ɒ/	hod
/tʃ/	check		catch	/ɔː/	hoard
/dʒ/	jump		cadge	/ʊ/	hood
/k,g/		rocky	bag	/3ː/	heard
/v/	very		have	/a/	hut
/θ/	thin		breath	/eɪ/	hate
/ð/	that		with	/əʊ/	hope
/z/			bars		
/ʃ/	show	station	cash		
/l/			mile		
/r/	red	berry			
/w/	wine				

The programme for the semester was as follows:

1. Introduction. Plans for making a video programme.
2. Meeting (teacher + students + technician).
   (a) Defining the *topic:*
       Business English:
       Danish textile firm making clothes in Hong Kong.
   (b) Discussing the cast.
   (c) Discussing the synopsis.
3. The students consider a full synopsis until next class meeting. 7-8 scenes.
4. Rehearsals. 8 scenes.
5. Final shooting.
6. Looking at the programme. Criticism.
   Discussion of improvements.
7. Evaluation.
8. How to use the programme afterwards.

Videodiscs

The development of the videodisc technique belongs to the 1980's, although it was introduced in the United States as early as in the late 70's. Anyone who has worked with videotape equipment and with videodisc systems as well, will realise the advantages of the latter. Among these advantages can be named:

1. The enormous storing capacity of an optical (laser-based) videodisc.
2. The endurance and quality.
3. The rapid random access mechanism.
4. The potential for microcomputer/video interface (the linking of a microcomputer to a videodisc unit).

The linking of a microcomputer and a videodisc gives the possibility for providing authentic examples of live environments to the user. The freeze-frame technique helps the students to answer questions and carry on a dialogue with the aid of his microcomputer. The computer can be programmed to select tasks according to the user's abilities and to generate questions according to the student's progress. Through generative programs such as this, it may be justifiable to speak of "intelligent" videodiscs.

There are, however, certain disadvantages to be considered. For example: the high costs involved. The first generation of optical videodiscs could not be updated. The new generation of magneto-optical laser videodiscs now includes that possibility.

The production of learning systems with videodiscs is very time-consuming and expensive. Therefore, there are to date very few available examples of language learning programmes based on the use of videodiscs. The so-called Montevidisco project developed at Brigham Young University, Utah, is perhaps the best known example. It is a computer-assisted interactive videodisc programme for learning Spanish. It is a simulation of a visit to a Mexican village, in which the student is exposed to a variety of life-like situations. The programme will be further described in Chapter 7 in connection with the discussion of simulation in language learning.

There is no doubt that the videodisc as an instructional tool in education will develop even further in the future both in terms of speed and of capacity. Since film, sound, text, still pictures, graphics, and more, can be stored and used with random access, we shall have at our disposal a system which is extremely flexible and which may be most useful for a very great variety of exercises and experiences in the areas of communicative training and simulation.

Bearing in mind what was said in Chapter 5 concerning the use of teletext and teleflashes, it is also pertinent to note that there are systems where teletext captions can be overlayed onto video pictures. It is also possible to link up with a viewdata database. The variety of an interactive video system thus becomes multiplied and enhanced. Used with discrimination and imagination, this technique will almost certainly prove to be effective for language learning.

One example of a successful interactive video system is CAVIS, developed at the West Sussex Institute of Higher Education, Bognor Regis, Sussex, England. This multi-media system is based on video-cassette pictures with text and teletext diagrams presented on a television screen. The sound and the video information are stored on a videocassette and texts and diagrams on a magnetic disc. See further P. Copeland, "An Interactive Video System for Education and Training", *British Journal of Educational Technology*, Vol. 14:1 (1983), pp. 59-65.

Some innovations in the video industry are particularly important.

Digital television is a recent innovation in video technology introduced by Matsushita Corporation, Japan, in 1984. In this system two images can be displayed on the screen at the same time, which can be most useful for educational purposes. High-definition television (HDTV) with three-dimensionality and great improvements in quality (much higher resolution) will probably also add to the educational advances.

Chapter 6: **Sources and further reading**

Brennan, M./ Miller, J.W. (1982), "Making an English language teaching videotape", *ELT Journal*, Vol. 36/3, April, pp. 169-74.

Calico Journal. Provo, Utah: Brigham Young University Press.

Candlin, C./ Charles, D./ Willis, J. (1982), *Video in English Language Teaching: an Inquiry into the Potential Uses of Video Recordings in the Teaching of English as a Foreign Language*. Gosta Green, Birmingham: University of Birmingham, Language Study Unit.

D'Antoni, S.G. (1982), "Videodisc and Videotex: New Media for Distance Education", in J.S. Daniel *et al.*, *Learning at a Distance*, pp. 287-90.

Duke, J. (1983), *Interactive Video: implications for education and training. Working Paper* 22. London: Council for Educational Technology.

v. Faber, H./ Eggers, D., eds. (1980), *Video im Fremdsprachenunterricht*. München: Goethe-Institut.

Förster, Hans-Peter (1982), *Video-mein Hobby*. München: Humboldt-Taschenbuchverlag.

Geddes, M./ Sturtridge, G. (1982), *Video in the Language Classroom*. London: Heinemann.

Jung, Udo, ed. (1985), *Man and the Media*. Proceedings of the AILA Symposium at Frankfurt; June 12-15, 1984.

Lavery, M. (1981), *Active Viewing: Video Exploitation Techniques in the Language Learning Classroom*. Canterbury: Pilgrims Publications.

Lonergan, J. (1984), *Video in Language Teaching*. Cambridge: Cambridge University Press.

McGovern, J., ed. (1983), *Video Applications in Language Teaching*. Oxford: Pergamon Press.

Molnar, A.R. (1983), "Intelligent videodisc and the learning society", *Journal of Computer Based Instruction*, 6. pp. 11-16

Sigel, E. *et al.* (1980), *Video Discs: The Technology, the Applications and the Future*. White Plains, New York: Knowledge Industry Publications, Inc.

System, the International Journal of Educational Technology and Language Learning Systems. Oxford: Pergamon Press.

Zettersten, A. (1983), *Business in Hong Kong. How to make your own video programme*. Copenhagen: Department of English.

Zuber-Skerrit, O., ed. (1983), *Video in Higher Education*. London: Kogan Page.

Chapter 7
Role-playing, simulation, drama, combinatory acquisition

Most recent books on the use of role-playing, simulation and drama in language learning have emphasized the importance of a communicative approach. See, for example, P. Watcyn-Jones (1978), and R. Clark – J. McDonagh (1982) for role-plays; K. Jones (1978) and J. Brims (1979) for simulation; and A. Maley – A. Duff (1978) and S. Holden (1981) for drama.

Most of the very imaginative and interesting ideas expressed by these authors can also be used in the context of the new technologies. This is particularly true of video and videodiscs. One example of the use of role-playing in practising language functions on video was given in Chapter 6 ("Business in Hong Kong"). That programme was an example of the technique of language training which I have called *combinatory acquisition,* which occurs when learners become absorbed in a specific problem-solving activity, lose their inhibitions concerning the target language, and therefore acquire better proficiency. It was my experience in the case of "Business in Hong Kong" that since the main task was to produce a video-programme based on a functional/notional approach, involving role-playing, simulation, and problem-solving, the language training activity of the teacher receded very much into the background. Maley (1983) describes what happens when meaningful and interesting activities are developed, observing that "absorption in the activity takes over from obsessive concern with the language." (p. 301).

One example of how role-playing can be used will be shown below. A student group at Copenhagen University were given the task of making a video film in two scenes about a drug addict. The students were asked to write a synopsis and to improvise on the basis of their synopsis in front of the cameras in the TV-studio. The synopsis looked like this:

Role-Play
A Short Play about Drug Dependence, Treatment and Rehabilitation.

Cast:

The addict .... Sanne
The doctor .... Hermod
The police woman .... Lotte
The leader of the rehabilitation centre .. Karen
The social worker .... Eva
The bartender/The boyfriend .... Finn
The waitress/The mother .... Grethe

Scene 1: In a bar at "Halmtorvet".
Characters: The doctor, the social worker and the leader of the centre discuss a film.

The addict interferes, she needs a fix badly, asks the doctor for help. The bartender interrupts the discussion. The leader of the centre and the social worker have different opinions as to the treatment of drug addiction. The question is whether the "patient" is genuinely addicted to such an extent that it is justifiable to prescribe methadone to help a gradual withdrawal and to "cure" the abstinence. Or if the "patient" needs psychiatric help or if group therapy is the best treatment in this case. Scene 1 ends with the three leaving together with the drug addict, who has agreed to come to the centre for treatment.

Scene 2: In a waiting room at the hospital.
Characters: The former addict and her boyfriend, the doctor, the leader of the centre, the social worker, the mother.

The addict has attempted suicide (an overdose). The boyfriend accuses the mother of having destroyed the daughter. General atmosphere of having failed in this case. A heated discussion follows. One by one the characters leave the room – the mother is having a nervous breakdown. We have to play this scene by ear.

The programme worked well and resulted in fruitful discussion and analysis afterwards. My view is that role-playing or simulation are much more effective if the activity can be recorded and analysed either by means of an audio-tape recorder or a video recorder. In either case the aspect of combinatory acquisition creates a situation which is learner-centred rather than teacher-centred.

A similar project was described by Maya Brennan and Janet Woodbury Miller of Zhongshan University, Guangzhou, China, in "Making an English Language Teaching Videotape", *ELT Journal*, 36/3 (1982), pp. 169-74. This article describes the work with the production of an English language teaching video-tape with university students in China. The programme described was titled "Seeing a Doctor in China." This tape could afterwards be used as teaching material, which adds a further dimension to the use of video recordings. The following programmes were also made: "Finding Your Way", "Eating Out", "The Moon Festival", "Making a Fianze" (a Chinese toy) and "Banking in China."

The advantages of role-playing in the training of communication have been widely documented. Peter Watcyn-Jones (1978), *Act English,* p. 9, emphasizes, among other things, the fact that role-play is a central issue in this context.

It is interesting to compare the ideas of combinatory acquisition with some methods of solving problems as a group activity using visual techniques which have developed in management training in American and German firms and organizations. The technique is called *moderation* and means that the learners are all responsible for the problem-solving together and the teacher acts as a kind of moderator. It has been suggested by Keith Purvis in his article "The Teacher as Moderator: A Technique for Interactional Learning", *ELT Journal*, 37/3 (1983), pp. 221-28, that this consultative technique could be useful for English language teaching.

According to this technique, participants write problems to be solved by group discussion on rectangular cards which are then collected by the moderator, who arranges them in clusters according to problem area. Explanations and objections that arise in the course of the discussion of the ideas are recorded on oval cards which are placed on a bulletin board together with the appropriate rectangular cards. Various interactional techniques are used both in large and small groups with different moderators and different problems.

This problem-solving technique used in management training can be very usefully applied to the training of communication skills. In order to reach a step further the activities should be tape-recorded or video-recorded for later analysis and greater feedback. Such an approach is an example of "learning by doing" in the spirit of Piaget.

My view is thus that one should try to go one step further than merely using role-playing, simulation, games, drama, and such techniques by themselves, through the use of the new technologies, which permit a much wider range of learning experiences by enabling the performances to be analysed, evaluated and discussed. The learning situation becomes enhanced by the addition of another dimension of experience in this way and also becomes more pleasurable and exciting for both students and teacher.

The technique of *simulation* has been used successfully in the teaching of various subjects at different educational levels for a number of years now. So far there is relatively little published research concerning its use in the teaching of foreign languages, but there is every reason to suppose that the technique can be very effectively applied to this area as well.

The essential idea of simulation is to represent a real-life situation in such a way that particular skills can be developed and trained. Types of simulation relevant to language learning include:

1. *The incident process:* in which the student is given certain information concerning an object or incident, and must obtain further information through asking relevant questions and receiving answers. Probably such games as "Twenty Questions" are the original model for this form of simulation. Conducted in the target language, this can be an interesting and effective method of training many aspects of language learning.
2. *Situation simulation:* the acting out by students of real-life situations, such as asking directions of a native of a foreign country, explaining the theft or loss of one's passport to a foreign policeman, accounting for certain personal possessions to a foreign customs agent. The possibilities are virtually endless.
3. *Game simulations:* the inter-action of a student with a simulated, structured environment. The range of possible games is very wide and can include anything from traditional games such as "Monopoly", for example, to complex real-life simulations such as saving a simulated developing country from famine by marshalling its resources.

The basic structure of simulations remains essentially the same however much their particular nature of length may vary. The first stage of a simulation should be devoted to the handing-out or transmission of the relevant information needed to execute the simulation. The second stage is the simulation itself. The third stage is the follow-up, in which the simulation is discussed, evaluated and analysed. This last stage provides valuable feedback.

Videodiscs and microcomputers have shown themselves to be highly effective in meeting the requirements of language learning simulators. They are especially effective when used in combination. The advantages of using them for simulators include: their economic feasibility in comparison to films and videotapes, the high degree of authenticity they convey, their precision and rapidity of function, and their adaptibility in terms of such enhancing devices as touch screens and voice input systems.

I have already mentioned the excellent "Montevidisco" simulation of a Mexican village, developed by Brigham Young University in Utah, which produces highly authentic language situations and permits genuine dialogue in Spanish. With the development of more such programmes, produced in a variety of languages and for various levels, a wide array of excellent, individualized teaching resources will become available. Programmes such as "Montevidisco" represent the next best thing to actual physical presence and speaking practice in a foreign country, and they are far less expensive.

"Montevidisco" is built up of 28 major sequences consisting of several scenes, each having at least four options. Altogether there are more than 1,100 options for the individual user. There is one version of "Montevidisco" for male students and one for female students due to the importance of gender in Spanish. The following list shows the main content of the two versions of one disc:

Male Scenes	Female Scenes
Introduction	Introduction
Tour guide	Meals
Market	Telephone
Hotel	Hotel room
Bull fight	Travel
Bus	Bus

Beach	Walking
Taxi	Taxi
Hospital	Library
Drug store	Drug store
Police station	Macho masher
Bar	Restaurant
Disco	Shopping
Plaza	Plaza

See further, Larrie E. Gale, "Montevidisco: An Anecdotal History of an Interactive Videodisc", *Calico Journal,* I:1 (1983), pp. 42-46.

The advantages of the various forms of simulation, whether carried out with existing classroom resources or with the aid of the new technologies include: the high degree of interest and involvement that they evoke from students; the opportunity for *combinatory acquisition* that they offer; the specificity of their intention (i.e. ordering a dinner, seeing a doctor, asking directions, reporting a theft, etc.); the flexibility of their level of difficulty; and their ability to be used on microcomputers and videodiscs, thus enabling individual students, distance-students and home-learners to have access to a selection of effective, interesting materials based on real-life discourse situations.

Readers interested in specific games and techniques are referred to Jacquetta Megarry's *Aspects of Simulation and Gaming* (1977); "Games in Language Teaching" by Adrian Palmer and Theodore S. Rodgers, *Simulations,* ELT Guide-2 (1979); and "Veni Vidi Vici Via Videodisc: A Simulator for Instructional Conversations" by Edward W. Schneider and Junius L. Bennion, *System,* Vol. 11, No. 1 (1983), pp. 41-46.

Chapter 7: **Sources and further reading**

Astrop, John/ Byrne, Donn (1981), *Games for Pairwork*. London: Modern English Publication.

Brumfit, C.J./ Johnson, K. (1973), *The Communicative Approach to Language Teaching*. London: Oxford University Press.

Byrne, D./ Rixon, S. (1979), *Communication games*. Windsor: NFER-Nelson.

Henderson, John/ Humphreys, Fay, eds. (1982), *Audio Visual and Microcomputer Handbook: the SCET Guide to Educational and Training Equipment*. London: Kogan Page.

Holden, Susan (1981), *Drama in Language Teaching*. Harlow: Longman.

Johnson, Keith/ Morrow, Keith, eds. (1981), *Communication in the Classroom*. London: Longman.

Jones, Ken (1978), *Simulations in Language Teaching*. Cambridge: Cambridge University Press.

Kleppin, Karin (1980), *Das Sprachlernspiel im Fremdsprachenunterricht: Untersuchungen zum Lehrer und Lernerverhalten im Sprachlernspiel*. Tübingen: Narr Verlag.

Lee, W.R. (1979), *Language-Teaching Games and Contests*. 2nd ed. Oxford: Oxford University Press.

Maley, Alan/ Duff, Alan (1978), *Drama Techniques in Language Learning*. Cambridge: Cambridge University Press.

Media in Education and Development, A Journal of the British Council. December 1983.

Omaggio, Alice C. (1979), *Games and Simulations in the Foreign Language Classroom*. Arlington, Va.: Center for Applied Linguistics, ERIC Clearinghouse on Languages and Linguistics.

Rixon, Shelagh (1981), *How to use games in Language Teaching*. Macmillan.

Sherrington, Richard (1973), *Television and Language Skills*. Oxford University Press.

Sigurd, B. (1982), "Commentator: a computer model of verbal production", *Linguistics* 20, pp. 611-32.

Watcyn-Jones, P. (1978), *Act English*. Harmondsworth: Penguin.

Wells, Gordon (1981), *Learning Through Interaction. The Study of Language Development*. Cambridge: Cambridge University Press.

Wright, Andrew/ Betterridge, David/ Buckby, Michael (1979), *Games for Language Learning*. Cambridge: Cambridge University Press.

Chapter 8
Artificial intelligence.
Synthetic speech. Robots

The literature on artificial intelligence has grown rapidly in volume in recent years. Several disciplines, including computer science, linguistics, philosophy, psychology, sociology and others, currently show a great interest in AI. It is, of course, still debatable what AI actually is, and whether a computer can or will be able to "think" independently, combine seemingly unrelated ideas, draw conclusions, produce unpredictable results, use imagination and other functions of human intelligence. The so-called fifth generation of computers is now being developed at Japan's Institute for New Generation Computer Technology (ICOT). The aim of this project is, among other things, to produce a generation of computers with a well-defined reasoning power. The computers should be able to draw conclusions from extensive knowledge bases and handle natural language.

Discussions of AI in connection with language programs have so far usually been carried out in connection with mainframe computers. Also, most experiments have been projects dealing with text comprehension, sentence parsing or pattern recognition rather than text production. Several word processing programs have been created. Some examples of programs showing an intelligent analysis of spelling, identifying and clarifying misspellings, have been written by Jørgen Christiansen of Copenhagen. It is also quite possible to use microcomputers for experiments on AI in connection with text production using a simple speech synthesizer called Votrax, as has been demonstrated by Bengt Sigurd, Lund University, Sweden. See further below.

There is still a degree of dispute concerning the precise nature of artificial intelligence. A comprehensive definition would be: the development of machines capable of heuristic approaches to problem solving; that is, approaches in which performance is improved upon on the basis of experience. A heuristic capability would enable a machine to carry out such functions as learning, reasoning, adaption, and self-correction.

One of the unique advantages of computer memory or intelligence is that it only contains what has been entered into it, it exists without preconceptions or predispositions. In this way, it is now believed that research currently in progress in the area of the use of computers in language comprehension may provide valuable insights into the language learning functions of the human brain, and may even provide a detailed model of the process of language acquisition. The usefulness of such a model would be immeasurable for structuring language instruction programmes and teaching materials. It should be emphasized that at present such research is as yet in its infancy. Potentially, though, it could represent a quantum jump in language learning.

Probably the best-known program developed to date is Terry Winograd's SHRDLU program in which such sentences as "Pick up the big red block and put it in the box", are converted into commands that are carried out by the computer. Within the parameters of the program (a simulated world containing a table, a box, various cubes and pyramids of different colours) questions may be answered, decisions made, mistakes corrected and reasons given on the basis of memory. The SHRDLU program is "self-referential" and is an important step toward an ultimate solution to what has been called "the problem of understanding understanding". See Winograd (1972), *Understanding Natural Language*.

For further reading on AI, the reader is referred to: Krutch (1981), *Experiments in Artificial Intelligence for Small Computers;* Winston (1981), *Artificial Intelligence;* Winograd (1983), *Language as a Cognitive Process*, Vol. I; and O'Shea-Self (1983), *Learning and Teaching with Computers: Artificial Intelligence in Education.*

A program developed on a micro-computer by Bengt Sigurd, Lund, called Commentator, provides a simulation of human behaviour in the context of commenting on situations or processes. The text production gives the user the possibility of studying the semantics of words, pronouns, sentence connectives, etc. The system is interesting for its connection with practical applications such as automatic commentators, talking robots, and more.

The sentences generated by the Commentator comment on the movements of two persons (actors) called, for example, Adam and Eve, moving around in front of a gate. A and E could also easily represent two boats hovering outside a harbour. With some imagination one would even see this simulation as the final scene of the medieval morality play called "Everyman" (=E) who is hovering outside his grave and finally it is only Good Deeds (=A) who is willing to accompany Everyman. The following picture (Figure 9) shows the position of A and E in relation to the gate (or harbour or grave). Small letters indicate previous positions of the persons.

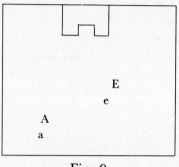

Fig. 9.

The text generated by the commentator in this case would be:

In Swedish: Adam är till vänster om Eva. Han är till vänster om porten också. Båda rör sig mot porten. Eva är närmast den dock.

In English: Adam is to the left of Eve. He is to the left of the gate too. Both are moving towards the gate. Eve is closest to it, however.

The following picture (Figure 10) shows the text production model underlying Commentator (after B. Sigurd, "Commentator: a computer model for verbal production", *Linguistics*, 20 (1982), p. 615).

Fig. 10.

A computer model of verbal production

Lines	Component	Task	Result (sample)
10-35	Primary information	Get values of primary dimensions	Localization coordinates
100-140	Secondary information	Derive values of complex dimensions	Distances, right-left, under-over
152-183	Focus and topicplanning expert	Determine objects in focus (referents) and topics according to menu	Choice of subject and objects and instructions to test abstract predicates with these
210-232	Verification expert	Test whether the conditions for the use of the abstract predicates are met in the situation (on the screen)	Positive or negative protosentences and instructions for how to proceed
500	Sentence-structure (syntax) expert	Order the abstract sentence constituents (subject, predicate, object); basic prosody	Sentence structure with further instructions
600-800-	Reference expert (subroutine)	Determine whether pronouns, proper nouns, or other expressions could be used	Pronouns, proper nouns, indefinite or finite NPs

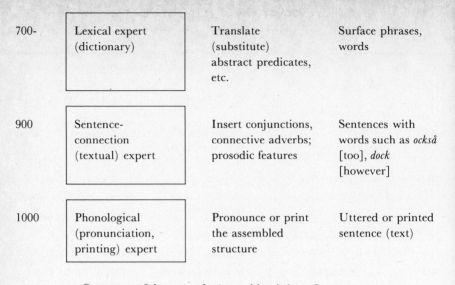

700-	Lexical expert (dictionary)	Translate (substitute) abstract predicates, etc.	Surface phrases, words
900	Sentence-connection (textual) expert	Insert conjunctions, connective adverbs; prosodic features	Sentences with words such as *också* [too], *dock* [however]
1000	Phonological (pronunciation, printing) expert	Pronounce or print the assembled structure	Uttered or printed sentence (text)

Components of the text-production model underlying Commentator

The Commentator system is interfaced with Votrax, the speech synthesizer that I mentioned above. Votrax can produce circa 60 American English sounds (allophones) and 4 pitch levels. It is self-evident that this inventory is not ideal for the production of Swedish speech. It is, however, quite surprising that the result is tolerably good, although some sounds such as the Swedish *u* and *y* are not accurate. It is also quite surprising that the pitch levels can be used for producing the Swedish word tones, accent 1 ("acute") as in *ánd-en* (=the duck) and accent 2 ("grave") as in *ànde-n* (= the spirit.)

The experiments mentioned above have a bearing on the discussion of talking robots, although it is not, at the present time, realistic to assume any practical use for robots in language learning situations. However, if one considers the potential of existing robots, it is certainly not inconceivable that many educational uses could be found for robots at some future time.

Voice synthesizers have also started to be used in programs designed for language learning in schools. This technique has been used particularly in spelling programs, in which a word is spoken as soon as it has been correctly spelt by the pupil. The so-called *talking typewriters* and text-to-speech systems (which can read text aloud) have also been in use for some time.

One area which has developed rather rapidly is the use of the *talking terminals* as a support for visually-handicapped students and learners. The Kurzweil optical scanner is perhaps the best known instrument into which a document can be inserted and a synthetic voice reads the text.

One computer-assisted learning system with interesting potentials was presented by A.G. Law, et al. in "Computer Voice Support for Visually-Handicapped Students", *Computer Education,* Vol. 8, No. 1, (1984) pp. 35-39. This article describes a system developed by the Mathesis Research and Development at the University of Regina in Saskatchewan, Canada, through which visually handicapped students can learn to program or to write an essay. The program is based on the use of a Votrax speech synthesizer which is managed by a microcomputer. In order to create the background for the programming analysis, a Braille flowcharting scheme was developed by the group as a substitute for the written flowcharts that are used by sighted students. Undoubtedly we may foresee further developments from a technical point of view in this research area, and further educational applications as well.

LOGO, a programming language developed by Seymour Papert, is a high-level language built up on instructions or codes which are words and numbers related to physical movements e.g. "Forward 15" (steps), "Write 90" (degrees). The program makes a Turtle move and draw geometrical patterns on the screen. A plastic robot turtle can also be attached to the computer by a cable to make the same movements. There is a pen attached to the Turtle by which students can write on a piece of paper on the floor. It has been particularly successful for lessons in geometry.

LOGO is designed to be used particularly by children. It has been reported by A. J. Obrist in his *The Microcomputer and the Primary School* (1983) that when children work in small teams with the Turtle there is "an enormous amount of discussion to the great benefit of the children's use of language" (p. 38). This is actually the ideal situation for *combinatory acquisition* to occur. The pupils learn communication in English at the same time as they learn how to use the computer language LOGO.

There are other robots on the market besides the Turtle, which is the best-known robot developed so far owing to the popularity of Seymour

Papert's book *Mindstorm: Children, Computers and Powerful Ideas* (1980) and the success of LOGO. There is one small robot called the *BBC Buggy*, which is designed for use in science classes, having a variety of sensors and programs. *Bigtrak* is another small robot quite different from the other two in that it has its own small microprocessor and a keypad on top. See Obrist (1983), pp. 38-41, 60.

I think that it may be appropriate here to emphasize that the educational potential of all of the above-named devices (AI, synthetic speech, robots) is not limited to special educational problems (such as those of the visually handicapped, for example) nor to the novelty appeal of these devices. Rather, such devices can have very broad educational application and far-reaching consequences for language learning and for learning in general. This is due to their ability to provide students with new perspectives on the subjects that are being studied, perspectives that often correspond to the very particular needs of individual students. In support of this contention, I would like to describe one of Papert's experiments which I find particularly significant.

A group of teen-age students of "average ability" were given the opportunity to study grammar through the use of computer programs that could generate sentences at random on the basis of chosen syntactic structures. The resulting "computer poetry" served to illustrate the functions of particular parts of speech in forming complete sentences. Papert describes the motivational transformation of one of the students, Jenny, who had previously been unable to distinguish or to understand the functions of nouns, verbs or adverbs, but who suddenly was able to do so. "She found herself classifying words into categories, not because she had been told she had to, but because she needed to. In order to "teach" her computer to make strings of words that looked like English, she had to "teach" it to choose words of an appropriate class." (Papert, p. 49).

Papert stresses that the degree of Jenny's excitement at her discovery was very high, because for the first time she saw the purpose of grammar, not merely the abstract purpose but the practical application. Papert goes on to report her transformation from a student who made low to average grades, to a "straight A" student for the remaining years of her education.

Granted that this story is only one example, but there are many more such reports from Papert and from other educators who have employed the new technologies in their various classroom disciplines. The potential is inherent in the new technologies to provide this rare and valuable sort of learning experience in which the practical and the abstract become united in personal discovery and the latent powers of each individual student can be released, encouraged, strengthened and brought to bear on the particular learning task at hand, whether it is language learning, geography or mathematics. This may ultimately prove to be the most fortunate aspect of the use of the new technologies in education. Computer-aided translations also come under the heading of AI, although a great deal of editing must sometimes be carried out by a translator. Microcat (published by Weidner Communications Corporation) and Alps (Automated Language Processing Systems) are two well-known American systems for computer-aided translations.

Chapter 8: **Sources and further reading**

Barr, A./ Feigenbaum, E., eds. (1981), *The Handbook of Artificial Intelligence*. Los Altos, California: William Kaufmann.

Billingsley, J. (1983), *DIY Robotics and Sensors with the BBC Computer*. London: Sunshine Books.

Billingsley, J. (1984), *DIY Robotics and Sensors on the Commodore Computer*. London: Sunshine Books.

Brain, K./ Brain, S. (1984), *Artificial Intelligence on the BBC and Electron*. London: Sunshine Books.

Feigenbaum, E.A./ McCorduck, P. (1983), *Artificial Intelligence and Japan's Computer Challenge to the World*. Amsterdam: Addison-Wesley.

Gevarter, W.B. (1982), *An Overview of Artificial Intelligence and Robotics*, Vol. 2: *Robotics*. U.S. Department of Commerce.

Krutch, J. (1981), *Experiments in Artificial Intelligence*. Indianapolis: Howard W. Sams.

Meredith, M.D./ Briggs, B.I. (1982), *Bigtrak Plus*. London: Council for Educational Technology.

Micro et Robots. Paris: La Société des Publications Radio – Electriques et Scientifiques.

Noss, R. (1983), *Starting LOGO*. Hatfield: AUCBE.

O'Shea, T./ Self, J. (1983), *Learning and Teaching with Computers*. Brighton: The Harvester Press.

Papert, S. (1980), *Mindstorms: Children, Computers and Powerful Ideas*. Brighton: The Harvester Press.

Rich, Elaine (1983), *Artificial Intelligence*. New York: McGraw-Hill.

Sigurd, B. (1982), "Commentator: a computer model of verbal production", *Linguistics*, 20, pp. 611-32.

Watt, D. (1983), *Learning With LOGO*. New York: McGraw-Hill.

Winograd, Terry (1983), *Language as a Cognitive Process*. Vol. I: Syntax. Reading, Mass.: Addison Wesley.

Winston, P. (1984), *Artificial Intelligence*. 2nd ed. Amsterdam: Addison-Wesley.

Chapter 9

The use of authentic material.
TV, film, video, radio, satellites

The resources of authentic material in the form of film and TV have been used by language teachers for a long time. It is, however, surprising that in proportion to the great number of useful films and TV programmes, there is so little additional material in the form of introductory exercises and tests and other supplementary materials. It is true that radio and TV courses in various countries have been very successful in the use of text-book instruction. In recent years some multimedia courses with TV programmes and text books as well as sound and video tapes have been based on a functional/notional approach, such as, for example, the BBC's "Follow Me".

Radio programmes with visual support, so called *radiovision*, have also been quite effective. Still, the authentic material which is available has not been utilized fully, and this is particularly true with regard to support materials.

There is a marked difference between *authentic materials* and *didactic materials*. In order to gain maximum access to real-life situations with natural and life-like communication, it is necessary to make use of available authentic documents. Philip Riley at the Centre de Recherches et d'Applications Pédagogiques en Langues (CRAPEL) at the University of Nancy in France, has given two definitions to an authentic document: (1) The first is a negative definition stating that it is "one which has not been produced for language learning or language teaching purposes". (2) The second is a positive definition stating that it is "one which has been produced in a real communication situation". Naturally, both are necessary to use in a language learning system. The BBC programme called "Panorama of the Week", which was cited and discussed in Chapter 5, is an example of authentic material with authentic discourse situations (interviews) between the sections of news reading.

If teachers or individual learners have access to a variety of good authentic documents, ancillary training and testing material can be quite easily produced according to certain fixed models. Some documents may have been produced for particular learning situations in disciplines other than language learning. Films produced for the purpose of teaching business administration, for example, may be suitable to use for learning English for specific courses (such as Business English). Such programmes may have a high degree of authenticity. This will be illustrated by some exercises and tests from a video programme originally intended to teach students about the balance sheet. The contents of the additional material produced for this programme, part of a course to teach Business English, are reproduced below:

1. Introduction.
2. A summary of the contents of the video programme.
3. Key-words in the programme. The most important terms used are presented.
4. Exercises and tests.
5. Word list.

All of the material except for the word list will be recorded here in order to fully illustrate how a learning package teaching both business administration and language can be developed. In view of what has been demonstrated in Chapter 3, it is obvious that the exercises could alternatively have been presented on a microcomputer.

Introduction

The material presented here can be used as an introduction to the video programme about the balance sheet. It is recommended that everyone read through the summary in English as well as all of the key words before seeing the film. It is also possible to read the introduction and the key words as homework.

After the students have seen the programme, the most difficult words and phrases may be practised with the aid of the exercises and tests. This, too, may be used as homework. The word list can be used both before and after the programme and also during the programme as the need arises. The video film was produced by Video Arts, England.

Summary of video programme

The idea of presenting this film to you is to teach you something about business administration and the most useful words and phrases connected with the *balance sheet*.

In the film about the balance sheet, a manager without formal education explains to a planning executive of a big multi-national company how business actually works. Ron Scroggs, the manager of Scroggs Manufacturing, owns a "wooden shed" in Brixton. He explains step by step to Mr. Julian Carruthers, the sophisticated manager, how to use a balance sheet, a profit and loss account, and a cash flow forecast.

It should be pointed out from the beginning that the balance sheet discussion is based on the English system, which is different in some respects from the Swedish.

Ron Scroggs starts by explaining where you get the money from when you set up a business. You get your money from two places. Firstly, you risk your own money, which we call *share capital*. Secondly, you can borrow some money, which we call *loan capital*. While there are two sources where money can come in from, there are also two places money can go out to. Firstly, you put some money into things you want to keep, such as buildings, machinery, etc. They are called *fixed assets*. Secondly, you can put it into things you want to sell, e.g. raw materials, packaging materials, etc. This is called *working capital*.

In order to explain more clearly what working capital is, Ron Scroggs takes some examples from Scroggs Manufacturing. The whole operation is described as a sort of cash merry-go-round. These practical examples make it easier to understand about the *overheads*.

The *profit and loss account* is also explained through practical examples. It was mentioned above that there are two places where money can come from. If your business starts making a profit we can name a third place. The profit can be put back into the business. This money is called *reserves* and is an entry in the IN-column.

There is also a third place – besides fixed assets and working capital – where money can go, namely *investments*.

If we sum up the complete balance sheet, the IN- and OUT-columns will be as follows

IN
1. share capital
2. loan capital
3. reserves

OUT
1. fixed assets
2. working capital
3. investments

The balance sheet tells you where your money is at present, whereas the P and L account tells you what happened to your money in the past. If you want to know where your money will be going in the future, you will have to look at a *cash flow forecast*.

It is quite obvious that Mr. Carruthers cannot start a business of his own until he has understood the following three important documents completely: balance sheet, profit and loss account, cash flow forecast.

Key-words *(English into Swedish)*

1.	balance sheet	= balansräkning
2.	turn over	= omsätta
3.	accounts	= räkenskaper
4.	management	= företagsledning
6.	profit and loss account	= resultaträkning
7.	cash flow forecast	= likviditetsprognos, -budget
8.	share capital	= aktiekapital
9.	shareholder	= aktieägare
10.	loan capital	= främmande kapital, lånekapital
11.	fixed assets	= anläggningstillgångar
12.	overheads	= fasta utgifter, övriga utgifter
13.	manufacturing labour	= tillverkningskostnader
14.	distribution labour	= distributionskostnader
15.	dividend	= utdelning
16.	current assets	= omsättningstillgångar
17.	current liabilities	= kortfristiga skulder

Exercise I *(Swedish into English)*

1. balansräkning = balance sheet
2. resultaträkning = profit and loss account
3. råmaterial = raw materials
4. rörelsekapital = working capital
5. anläggningstillgångar = fixed assets
6. omsättningstillgångar = current assets
7. kortfristiga skulder = current liabilities
8. kontantflöde = cash flow
9. likviditetsbudget = cash flow forecast
10. aktiekapital = share capital
11. lånekapital = loan capital
12. främmande kapital = loan capital

Exercise II *(Swedish into English)*

13. eget kapital = share capital
14. fasta utgifter = overheads
15. aktieägare = shareholder
16. utdelning = dividend
17. vinst = profit
18. förlust = loss
19. räkenskapar = accounts
20. övriga utgifter = overheads
21. balansräkning = balance sheet
22. resultaträkning = profit and loss account
23. bolagsskatt = corporation tax
24. kortfristiga skulder = current liabilities

Exercise III *(Swedish into English)*

25. aktiekapital = share capital
26. eget kapital = share capital
27. omsättningstillgångar = current assets
28. anläggningstillgångar = fixed assets
29. främmande kapital = loan capital
30. utdelning = dividend
31. rörelsekapital = working capital
32. balansräkning = balance sheet
33. aktieägare = shareholder
34. resultaträkning = profit and loss account
35. lånekapital = loan capital
36. vinst = profit

Exercise IV

After the six words in the left margin, four suggestions for the corresponding meaning in Swedish are given, of which only *one* is correct. Mark at the bottom of the pages which alternative (A, B, C or D) you consider the best.

		A	B	C	D
1.	balance sheet	räkenskaper	resultaträkning	balansräkning	fasta utgifter
2.	profit and loss account	kortfristiga skulder	resultaträkning	räkenskaper	konkursredovisning
3.	share capital	lånekapital	aktieägare	främmande kapital	aktiekapital
4.	shareholder	aktiekapital	aktieägare	lånekapital	deltagare
5.	dividend	utdelning	omsättning	resultaträkning	fasta utgifter
6.	overheads	räkenskaper	projektor	övriga utgifter	utdelning

Fill in your answers below (A, B, C or D). If you feel uncertain, make an attempt all the same. Turn to the following page for the correct answers.

1. balance sheet   =
2. profit and loss account =
3. share capital   =
4. shareholder   =
5. dividend   =
6. overheads   =

Correct answers:

1. balance sheet   : C
2. profit and loss account : B
3. share capital   : D
4. shareholder   : B
5. dividend   : A
6. overheads   : C

Repeat the vocabulary exercise by masking the correct answers below:

1. balance sheet   = balansräkning
2. profit and loss account = resultaträkning
3. share capital   = aktiekapital
4. share holder   = aktieägare
5. dividend   = utdelning
6. overheads   = fasta utgifter, övriga utgifter

Exercise V

After the six words in the left margin, four suggestions for the corresponding meaning in Swedish are given, of which only *one* is correct. Mark at the bottom of the pages which alternative (A, B, C or D) you consider the best.

	A	B	C	D
1. turn over	distribuera	balansera	omsätta	dela ut
2. management	företagsledning	utdelning	balansräkning	aktiekapital
3. loan capital	lånekostnader	aktiekapital	resultaträkning	lånekapital
4. fixed assets	bestämda utgifter	anläggningstillgångar	tillverkningskostnader	omsättningstillgångar
5. current liabilities	tillverkningskostnader	omsättningstillgångar	resultaträkning	kortfristiga skulder
6. accounts	vinst	räkenskaper	utdelning	distributionskostnader

Fill in your answers below (A, B, C or D). If you feel uncertain, make an attempt all the same. Turn to the following page for the correct answers.

1. turn over   =
2. management   =
3. loan capital   =
4. fixed assets   =
5. current liabilities   =
6. accounts   =

Correct answers:

1. turn over   : C
2. management   : A
3. loan capital   : D
4. fixed assets   : B
5. current liabilities   : D
6. accounts   : B

Repeat the vocabulary exercise by masking the correct answers below:

1. turn over   = omsätta
2. management   = företagsledning
3. loan capital   = lånekapital, främmande kapital
4. fixed assets   = anläggningstillgångar
5. current liabilities   = kortfristiga skulder
6. accounts   = räkenskaper

Exercise VI

After the six words in the left margin, four suggestions for the corresponding meaning in Swedish are given, of which only *one* is correct. Mark at the bottom of the pages which alternative (A, B, C or D) you consider the best.

	A	B	C	D
1. cash flow forecast	fasta utgifter	framtidsutsikter	likviditetsprognos	kontantinsats
2. current liabilities	kortfristiga skulder	tillverkningskostnader	omsättningstillgångar	löpande räkning
3. profit and loss account	vinstfördelning	resultaträkning	utdelning	kortfristiga skulder
4. current assets	kortfristiga skulder	omsättning	löpande räkning	omsättningstillgångar
5. manufacturing labour	distributionskostnader	extraarbete	framställningskonst	tillverkningskostnader
6. loan capital	lånekostnader	främmande kapital	aktiekapital	startkapital

Fill in your answers below (A, B, C or D). If you feel uncertain, make an attempt all the same. Turn to the following page for the correct answers.

1. cash flow forecast   =
2. current liabilities   =
3. profit and loss account   =
4. current assets   =
5. manufacturing labour   =
6. loan capital   =

Correct answers:

1. cash flow forecast   : C
2. current liabilities   : A
3. profit and loss account   : B
4. current assets   : D
5. manufacturing labour   : D
6. loan capital   : B

Repeat the vocabulary exercise by masking the correct answers below:

1. cash flow forecast   =   likviditetsprognos, -budget
2. current liabilities   =   kortfristiga skulder
3. profit and loss account   =   resultaträkning
4. current assets   =   omsättningstillgångar
5. manufacturing labour   =   tillverkningskostnader
6. loan capital   =   främmande kapital, lånekapital

Exercise VII

Insert the correct word or phrase in the corresponding gap below:

fixed assets   balance sheet
dividend   profit and loss account
overheads   management
current assets   cash flow forecast
share capital   current liabilities

1.	=	utdelning
2.	=	aktiekapital
3.	=	anläggningstillgångar
4.	=	resultaträkning
5.	=	företagsledning
6.	=	likviditetsprognos
7.	=	fasta utgifter
8.	=	omsättningstillgångar
9.	=	balansräkning
10	=	kortfristiga skulder

Check among the key-words for your score.

Exercise VIII

Insert the correct word or phrase in the corresponding gap below:

deputy executive   merry-go-round
working capital   creditor
accountant   rates
cash flow   equity
alloy   turn-over (sb.)

1.	=	kontantflöde (I)
2.	=	kommunalskatter (X)
3.	=	biträdande chef (I)
4.	=	omsättning (I)
5.	=	karusell (XIII)
6.	=	stamaktier (IV)
7.	=	rörelsekapital (I)
8.	=	fordringsägare (XV)
9.	=	kamrer (I)
10.	=	legering (VIII)

Check the meanings of the words in the glossary. After each word there is a figure referring to the section in the glossary to which the word belongs.

Exercise IX

One of the three alternatives below represents the correct translation of the word or phrase to the left. Indicate the correct answer and then check afterwards among the key-words.

1. fixed assets
   - ☐ a) fasta utgifter
   - ☐ b) anläggningstillgångar
   - ☐ c) främmande kapital

2. current assets
   - ☐ a) lånekapital
   - ☐ b) aktiekapital
   - ☐ c) omsättningtillgångar

3. current liabilities
   - ☐ a) kortfristiga skulder
   - ☐ b) fasta utgifter
   - ☐ c) löpande räkning

4. overheads
   - ☐ a) utdelning
   - ☐ b) övriga utgifter
   - ☐ c) räkenskaper

5. cash flow forecast
   - ☐ a) likividitetsbudget
   - ☐ b) främmande kapital
   - ☐ c) resultaträkning

6. manufacturing labour
   - ☐ a) distributionskostnader
   - ☐ b) företagsledning
   - ☐ c) tillverkningskostnader

Exercise X

Insert the correct word or phrase in the corresponding gap below:

account	accountant
management	alloy
shareholder	overheads
stamp	fixed assets
consignment	dividend

1.	=	utdelning (XXII)
2.	=	fasta utgifter (X)
3.	=	stansa (XII)
4.	=	legering (VIII)
5.	=	sändning (XVIII)
6.	=	räkenskaper (I)
7.	=	företagsledning (I)
8.	=	aktieägare (IV)
9.	=	kamrer (I)
10.	=	anläggningstillgångar (VI)

Check the meanings of the words in the glossary. After each word there is a figure referring to the section in the glossary to which the word belongs.

Similar exercises may be used in connection with radio and TV programmes, films and video, as well as interactive videodisc programmes. When greater numbers of people gain access to satellite TV the selection of authentic documents will be even richer. The advantage of learning about, for example, the balance sheet at the same time as learning English for specific purposes is similar to what is gained by combinatory acquisition (see Chapter 6). In fact, the idea of combining two learning situations could be developed even further. The students could be asked to produce their own support materials based on certain fixed models. Discussing methods and techniques for writing this material for learning both about the balance sheet and about LSP will make the training of communication more natural and more meaningful.

There are, of course, various ways in which a teacher or a learner can find useful support material through already existing courseware. Some of the techniques of using such materials are discussed in a special issue of the *British Journal of Language Teaching*, Vol. XVIII: 2-3 (1980), dealing with "The Use of Broadcast Material in Language Teaching."

Radiovision, which was mentioned above, provides material which consists of:

1. A double-frame colour filmstrip.
2. Radiovision Teacher's Notes, containing the full text of the radio programme and hints on how to use the broadcast.
3. The soundtrack which has to be recorded from the radio.

(See P. Brooke, "Radiovision in Modern Language Teaching", in the above mentioned issue of the *British Journal of Language Teaching*). In the same issue there is an article on "How Television can help the Modern Language Teacher" (pp. 120-128) by Mary Law, and one on "A Multi-media Approach to Language Teaching: Variations on a Theme" by P.J. Downes. In the latter article some practical examples are given concerning how television can be used with support materials. The following is an example of one way in which television can be used for learning French as a second language. In this instance the topic is "Shopping for Food" (pp. 130-131). The following components are recommended:

1. Flashcards to present the main lexical items.
2. Filmstrip and tape recording to bring lexical items into context.
3. Cassette recording of conversations printed in the Pupil's Book, belonging to the course.
4. Pupil's Book and workbook exercises.
5. Language-laboratory exercises.
6. Selections from other TV programmes with the same topic.
7. Colour slides for detailed study of shops, etc.

Downes (p. 130) advocates the view that "the teacher's main task is to *select* from the programmes available, using them as a resource bank, those sequences which will support and exemplify whatever he is teaching in his basic course or syllabus." The author also mentions the fact that students are becoming increasingly critical of television in the sense that their interest will not be engaged by boring or amateurish productions. The selection of materials should therefore be carefully planned, each element screened and evaluated for its general quality and effectiveness.

In conjunction with the use of visual materials it may also be profitable to introduce media analysis. Various ways of achieving "teleliteracy" have been suggested by Len Masterman in his *Teaching about Television* (1982). A student's understanding of the target language may be enhanced by his/her appreciation of other visual codes which are closely related to linguistic expression. These visual codes include:

1. The codes of expression. Understanding the meaning of facial expressions.
2. The codes of gesture. Understanding the meaning of posture, gesture, body-language.
3. The codes of clothing. Understanding the meaning of costume.

In addition, certain technical codes of visual communication may be discussed, including the codes of objects and backgrounds, the codes of technique (camera angle, picture quality, distance, etc.) and iconographic analysis of the content of images.

Another technique of storing authentic material is to make use of the dense storage capacity of the interactive videodisc. Those who have access to a selection of authentic slides showing people or places, may transfer these automatically to videotape or film. The advantage of the random accessibility of the videodisc is, in this case, particularly great. This automatic transfer of still images has been described by Michael DeBloois in "Single Frame Video for Language Instruction", *Calico Journal*, I:1, September 1983, pp. 7-9.

The author here draws attention to the use of a still-frame audio adaptor in this connection. The videodisc is in this instance able to provide up to 70 seconds of audio with every single frame of video. It is clear that with the combination of music, motion, sound and computer text, some very exciting foreign language simulations can be produced.

The use of authentic material in the manner in which it has been described in the foregoing, would be particularly interesting and effective in the context of a functional/notional approach.

The need for more and more authentic material in the future will probably be satisfied quite easily with the expansion of cable links for television. The modern geo-stationary satellites are so powerful that they cover several countries, which facilitates the transmission of authentic documents for language learning purposes from one country to another. Through the increasingly widespread network of satellites numerous channels may be in operation and the material further distributed through cable companies. It is likely that the wideband cables which will be used in the future will be optic fibre cables, through which information will be optically transmitted. One innovation which will be quite revolutionary for educational and informational purposes is two-way TV communication. The implications for distance education in language learning should be particularly emphasized.

Chapter 9: **Sources and further reading**

British Broadcasting Corporation (1978), *Adults learning foreign languages: the role of BBC broadcasting*, by Neil Barnes. London: BBC.

Bufe, W./ Deichsel, J./ Dethloff, U. (1984), *Fernsehen und Fremdsprachenlernen*. Tübingen: Gunter Narr Verlag.

Hill, Brian (1981), *Some applications of media technology to the teaching and learning of languages. Language Teaching and Linguistics: Abstracts*, Vol. 14, No. 3, pp. 147-161.

Media in Education and Development, A Journal of the British Council, December 1983.

Ryback, S. (1980), *Learning languages from the BBC: research into courses*. London: BBC.

Sherrington, Richard (1973), *Television and Language Skills*. Oxford University Press.

The Use of Broadcast Material in Language Teaching (1980), A special edition of Volume 18, Nos. 2 & 3 of the *British Journal of Language Teaching*.

Watson, J./ Hill, A. (1984), *A Dictionary of Communication and Media Studies*. London: Edward Arnold Ltd.

Wegner, H. (1977), *Feature films in second language instruction*. Arlington, Va: Center for Applied Linguistics.

Chapter 10
The use of telephone exercises.
Teleconferencing.
Satellite communication

So far the use of the telephone in language learning has only been touched on in connection with viewdata systems described in chapter 4. In that context the telephone was only used as a technical link in the system. The telephone as a self-supporting aid in language education has been used quite extensively, especially in the United States. See, for example, L.A. Parker-B. Riccomini (1977), *The Telephone in Education*. Telephone tutoring has been used as a supplement to correspondence education in schools, universities and institutes for distance education. It was reported by R. Flinck in his *Correspondence Education Combined with Systematic Telephone Tutoring* (1978), that in the Swedish experimental study of the use of telephone tutoring in the teaching of French, the group that had received telephone tutoring achieved higher scores than the control group when taking the final test.

In LSP courses for businessmen, I had the opportunity of studying how telephone tutoring had a positive effect on the degree of language proficiency in English. In the system that I devised for Liber Hermods intensive courses in English in Malmö, Sweden, it was clear that telephone tutoring served as a strong reinforcement factor in an LSP course, if the intensive teaching days were spread over a period of several months rather than being placed together in an intensive period of one or two weeks, as is the usual practice in intensive language courses. The telephone periods of usually half an hour served as communication exercises, in which some of the exercises practised at the intensive face-to-face meetings could be repeated or followed up, and preparations for the following face-to-face meeting could be made.

Some specific language functions such as greetings, leave-taking, asking, accepting an order or invitation, suggesting a course of action, requesting others to do something, etc., could be practised more naturally than if the same situations had been simulated at a face-to-face meeting. These authentic telephone exercises were examples of a kind of combinatory acquisition. The students learnt specific language functions while at the same time learning to handle the specific telephone technique of each simulated situation. It should be stressed that a high degree of authenticity is required to make telephone simulations truly effective. The more specific and life-like the simulation is, the more likelihood there is of language functions being successfully trained and of combinatory acquisition taking place.

In the Copenhagen video experiment reported in chapter 6, the use of the telephone was also an important part of the simulation. In that experiment an LSP exercise, "Business in Hong Kong", was recorded on video and the language functions were discussed and analysed after the programme was finished. In this case telephone exercises could be recorded on the videotape with both speakers seen at the same time using only half of the screen each. The viewers analysing a telephone scene could thus study the two businessmen, one from Copenhagen and one from Hong Kong, simultaneously and could evaluate their performance. The following list shows the language functions used in the first scene of the video experiment "Business in Hong Kong."

SCENE 1

LANGUAGE FUNCTION

I.1   Identifying
I.2   Asking
II.2   Accepting an offer or invitation
II.3   Inquiring whether something is possible or impossible
III.3   Expressing interest or lack of interest
III.7   Expressing want, desire
VI.1   Greeting people

I.2   Asking
III.7   Expressing want, desire
IV.1   Expressing approval
V.1   Suggesting a course of action
V.2   Requesting another to do something

Teaching telephone conversation is often a neglected area in LSP courses and in distance education, although there are various models available. See, for example, Cripwell (1981), *On the Line*. One way of teaching telephone conversation in a system of distance education was the following synopsis for a course which was intended for a new interactive course for the Open University in Thailand.

English on the Telephone

I.   *Introduction*. Description of techniques of telephoning. Purpose of the course, special difficulties for Thai speakers of English, such as final consonants, clusters. Cultural aspects. Interference from Thai. Suggestions for individual training.

II. *Key words in telephoning*. Switch board, extension, exchange, operator, long-distance call, collect call (Am.).

III. *The alphabet*.
     A for Apple, B for Bangkok, C for cat, D for _____

Scene I

A. My name is _____ I would like to talk to Mr. _____, please.

B. I am sorry, I did not quite catch your name.

A. My name is _____ I would like to speak with Mr. _____

B. I am very sorry, but could you spell your name, please.

_____

_____

IV. Glossary of telephone words.

Plan

A. Either *one booklet* + *one tape* with 15 scenes.
    or

120

B. One booklet with one tape (general telephone English) with 7 scenes (interaction) and one booklet with one tape (business English) with 8 scenes.

Scenes

1. Spelling your name.
2. Calling a foreign guest at a hotel in Bangkok.
3. Calling a business contact to discuss a meeting.
4. Leave-taking. Calling a foreign guest before he is due to leave Bangkok.
5. Booking a hotel room in Hong Kong.
6. Booking a seat on a flight from Hong Kong to Bangkok.
7. A long-distance call to a friend in Singapore.
8. An international call to America. Spelling the name. Leaving a message for later contact.
9. A call to America. Discussing a meeting in Bangkok.
10. Calling a foreign friend to discuss the coming week-end.
11. A call to make enquiries about an advertisement.
12. In a hotel in Kuala Lumpur: order a meal by room service.
13. In Hong Kong: ordering a table for two at a restaurant.
14. Calling a Hong Kong bank to order some traveller's cheques. (Exchange rates).
15. Calling a travel agency in Hong Kong.
16. Calling the wrong number.

If video cameras are available in a learning situation, then it is quite obvious that recording exercises such as those shown above may create excellent feedback for the participants. In actual practice such occurrences as voice-lag, voice distortion and poor telephone connections can make long-distance business conversations difficult, and even more difficult for non-native speakers. There is, consequently, a need for intensive training in telephone conversation, particularly in LSP courses for businessmen.

Teleconferencing

It is important to mention *teleconferencing* in this context. It has grown in popularity quite rapidly and, although its main purpose is to alleviate the problems of business meetings and save time and travelling, it is very easy to realize the excellent possibilities for teaching communication which are inherent in this medium. In his paper "Continuing Education Resources for Electronics-Based High Technology R & D Professionals: Part One: Overview", *Educational Technology*, November 1981, p. 18, L.S. Menashian distinguishes between four major types of teleconferencing:

1. *Audio teleconferencing*, which is the cheapest and most commonly used technique.
2. *Video teleconferencing*, of which there are two different types, one of which may be called *slow-scan* and the other *full-motion*. With the former type, still pictures are shown on a monitor. The latter type is a full television broadcast of a meeting and complete two-way communication can thus be practised and afterwards analysed.
3. *Computer-based teleconferencing* is both individual and interactive. The participants need not be present at a meeting at the same time but can leave their messages, look through the answers later and reply at any time of the day.
4. The fourth technique is a mixture of two of the above-mentioned types, usually called a *media mix*. Sometimes this media mix may be supplemented by further educational media, such as text, slides, audiotapes and videotapes.

Three successful examples of teleconference applications in education will be mentioned below. The first is the University of Wisconsin Extension Educational Telephone Network (ETN) which has offered courses to university campuses, hospitals, libraries, etc., in many subjects. For a description of these courses, see Johansen-McNulty-McNeal (1978), *Electronic Education: Using Teleconferencing in Postsecondary Organizations*. There are also plans in Britain for a similar Open University Teleconferencing Network (OUTNET). See M. More, "Educational Telephone Networks", *Teaching at a Distance,* 19 (1981), p. 29.

The second application is a joint venture called the Carleton-Stanford Universities' Curriculum Exchange, using the Canadian Communication Technology Satellite. Students at Stanford University in California, USA, and at Carleton University in Ottawa, Canada, can take part in each others' courses. Both two-way audio and video are used and full interaction in the courses is achieved.

In the University of Alberta Research Project, Alberta, Canada, the results showed that television group conferencing was just as effective as face-to-face instruction.

Satellite technology opens up many interesting perspectives, particularly in continuing education. The future use of optical fibres will, as has been mentioned previously, increase two-way communication in education. So much more information will be able to be transmitted via laser beams, that multimedia systems can be set up in educational contexts.

BIGFON (= Breitbandiges integriertes Glasfaser-Fernmelde-Ortsnetz) is a future broadband communication system in the Federal Republic of Germany.

The BIGFON system shown in Figure 11 which also includes the TV telephone, has been adapted from the BIGFON system depicted in H.P. Förster (1982), *Video – Mein Hobby,* p. 43.

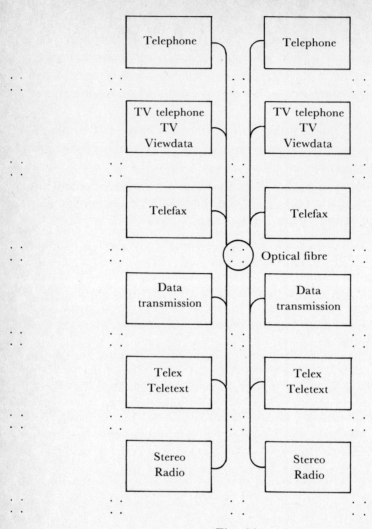

Fig. 11.

Chapter 10: **Sources and further reading**

Bacsich, P.D. (1982), *Audio-Videotex Teleconferencing*. Milton Keynes: Open University.

Beck, I.M./ Odeldahl, A. (1977), *Telefonengelska*. Stockholm: Esselte Studium.

Cripwell, Ken (1981), *On the Line*. London: Oxford University Press.

Curtis, J./ Biedenbach, J., eds. (1979), *Educational Telecommunications Delivery Systems*. Washington, D.C.

Flinck, R. (1978), *Correspondence Education Combined with Systematic Telephone Tutoring*. Malmö: Hermods.

Gruebel, J./ Robinson, W.N./ Rutledge, S. (1980), *Directory of Intrastate Educational Telecommunication Systems*. Washington, D.C.

Gruebel, J./ Robinson, W.N./ Rutledge, S. (1981), "Intrastate Educational Telecommunication Systems: A National Survey", *Educational Technology*, April, pp. 33-36.

Hudson, L./ Bunting, D. (1982), "The Telenetwork System: A Viable Alternative for Delivering Distant Instruction", *Educational Technology*, August, pp. 17-19.

Johansen/ McNulty/ McNeal (1978), *Electronic Education: Using Teleconferencing in Postsecondary Organizations*.

Kirman, J.M./ Goldberg, J. (1981), "Distance Education: Teacher Training Via Live Television and Concurrent Group Telephone Conferencing", *Educational Technology*, April, pp. 41-42.

Moore, M. (1981), "Educational Telephone Networks", *Teaching at a Distance*, 19, pp. 29-31.

Olgren, C.H./ Parker, L.A. (1983), *Teleconferencing, Technology and Application*. Dedham MA: Artech House Inc.

Parker, L.A./ Monson, M.K. (1980), *Teletechniques: An Instructional Model for Interactive Teleconferencing*. Englewood Cliffs, N.J.

Parker. L.A./ Riccomini, B., eds. (1977), *The Telephone in Education*. Madison, Wisconsin.

Teleconferencing. CET Information Sheet No. 7 (October 1983). London: Council for Educational Technology.

Teleconferencing and Electronic Communication. Vol. I (1982), Vol. II (1983). University of Wisconsin: Center for Interactive Programs.

Thompson, G. (1984), "The Development of the Educational Telephone Network at the University of Wisconsin", *ICDE, International Council for Distance Education*, Vol. 5, pp. 47-52.

Chapter 11

Language testing.
Distance testing. Self-testing

Language testing with the aid of computers has been practised for a considerable time. Most of the statistical calculations presented in books and articles on language testing in the 1960's, 70's, and 80's could not have been carried out without extensive use of mainframe computers.

There are many areas of language testing where the use of computers is extremely helpful, such as optical scanning, item analysis, reliability, validity, standard deviation, correlation analysis, Rasch modelling, implicational scaling, etc. Methods in which the computer can be used for statistical calculation can be seen in E. Hatch/H. Farhady (1982), *Research Design and Statistics for Applied Linguistics*. In this chapter some experiments will be presented which have not been widely discussed previously. The first area of experimentation is distance education (with the aid of mainframe computers) and the second is self-testing (with the aid of microcomputers, viewdata and teletext).

In the first experiment with large-scale vocabulary testing, the computer was used for calculating the scoring, the statistical tables and the item analysis. The model used in the Nordic countries was later used in China. The last five items of this test are recorded below:

Fig. 12.

Danish:

		A:	B:	C:	D:	E:
116.	REAL ESTATE	ejendom	salgsværdi	stor udstrækning	virkelighed	årsindtægt
117.	SEEMLY	ganske	kræsen	passende	tilsyneladende	sandsynligt
118.	SQUALL	aftenringning	affald	flyde	byge	sladder
119.	SWATHE	indhylle	skum	svaje	sved	svæve
120.	TREACLE	dryppe	sirup	sladre	spæk	trefoldig

Finnish:

		A:	B:	C:	D:	E:
116.	REAL ESTATE	kinteistö	maan arvo	laajuus	todellisuus	vuositulo
117.	SEEMLY	melko	vaatelias	sopiva	nähtävästi	luultavasti
118.	SQUALL	iltasoitto	jätteet	virrata	sadekuuro	juoru
119.	SWATHE	kääriä	vaahto	sorvata	hiki	liidellä
120.	TREACLE	tippua	siirappi	lörpötellä	silava	kolminkertainen

Norwegian:

		A:	B:	C:	D:	E:
116.	REAL ESTATE	eiendom	salgsverdi	stor utstrekning	virkelighet	årsinntekt
117.	SEEMLY	temmelig	kresen	passende	tilsynelatende	sannsynlig
118.	SQUALL	aftenringning	avfall	flyte	byge	sladder
119.	SWATHE	svøpe inn	skum	svaie	svette	sveve
120.	TREACLE	dryppe	sirup	sladre	fett	trefoldig

Swedish:

		A:	B:	C:	D:	E:
116.	REAL ESTATE	fastighet	markvärde	stor utsträckning	verklighet	årsinkomst
117.	SEEMLY	ganska	kräsen	passande	tillsynes	trolig
118.	SQUALL	aftonringning	avskräde	flöda	regnby	skvaller
119.	SWATHE	linda in	lödder	svarva	svett	skvaller
120.	TREACLE	drypa	sirap	sladdra	späck	trefaldig

The purpose of the experiment was to compare the English vocabulary proficiency of first-year students of English in Denmark, Finland, Norway and Sweden. In addition to the various statistical results given by the computer programme, I took great interest in the item analysis, with a view to criticizing my own choice of test words as much as possible.

The best known cross-national study of achievement in English connected with Scandinavia is the project organized by the International Association for the Evaluation of Educational Achievement (IEA), which was started in 1965 and comprised intensive research in ten countries for about seven years. The participating countries were Belgium (French region), Chile, the Federal Republic of Germany, Finland, Hungary, Israel, Italy, the Netherlands, Sweden, and Thailand. This study was part of a comprehensive programme which examined six major subject areas – Science, Reading Comprehension, Literature, Civics Education, French as a Foreign Language, and English as a Foreign Language – in over 20 countries. The aim of this extensive study was to examine the differences in achievement between students, schools and countries.

One of the results shown by the English study was "that cross-national comparisons of achievement in English are possible provided that great care is taken in the construction of the instruments" (Lewis-Massad 1975:296). This statement may seem self-evident, but it is also necessary to emphasize the fact that not only the test instruments but also the types of data analysed in a cross-sectional study must be identical or nearly identical.

My own distance-learning experiment (fig. 12) was a multiple-choice test scored by computer. The test consists of 120 English words divided into six different groups corresponding to six different frequency bands of English words. These frequency bands are related to different school levels. For each English word there are five different translations (or choices), one of which is correct. This one, called the key, is definitely correct or more suitable than the others. The choice that the scorer assumes is the correct one is marked on an answer sheet which is read by an optical scanner.

The computer program provides the following statistics:
1. A survey of answers given, numbers of correct answers, scores and

z-scores. The z-score is a standard score where the mean is 0 and the standard deviation is 1.

2. A survey showing the right or wrong answers of the individual students.
3. The results of six sub-groups.
4. A survey showing:
   Number of students
   Number of parts or sub-groups
   Number of questions (total no. and no. for each sub-group)
   Grading of the importance of the individual sub-group
   Mean score
   Standard deviation
   Maximum result
   Minimum result
   K - R (20) = the Kuder - Richardson formula 20, which is a reliability coefficient.
5. Histogram showing the distribution of the z-scores.
6. Item analysis indicating percentage of answers for each of the five alternatives under each item. A discrimination coefficient, R(P - BIS), for each item is also indicated.

The test was given to various student groups in the Nordic countries. Some Danish teachers' training colleges and schools were tested in the same period.

The investigation can therefore be divided into two parts, namely:

I. *Cross-national comparison,* showing the results of the main study, i.e. the vocabulary proficiency of students of English at universities in Denmark, Finland, Norway, and Sweden.

II. *National comparisons,* showing the results of certain pilot studies in schools and teachers' training colleges in Denmark and from distance education in Sweden.

The investigation gave the following results, i.e. the following average raw scores were reached by the groups under study.

I. Cross-national comparisons

University of Copenhagen, Denmark	65.4
University of Jyväskylä, Finland	64.5
Åbo Akademi, Finland	60.0
University of Oslo, Norway	67.8
University of Lund, Sweden	69.7

II. National comparisons
Denmark:

Royal Danish School of Educational Studies	80.5
Blågård Teachers' Training College 3 II	63.8
Blågård Teachers' Training College 2 II	65.8
Frederiksberg Teachers' Training College	47.4
Herlev State Grammar School	41.3
Rødovre Statsskole, Language Stream	38.8
Rødovre Statsskole, Mathematics Stream	36.0
Rødovre Statsskole, Higher Preliminary Examination	29.9

Sweden:

Distance Education, Hermods, course A1	77.7
Distance Education, Hermods, course AB 1	88.2

The conclusion drawn from the cross-national comparison is that the first-year students of English in Denmark, Finland, Norway, and Sweden have roughly the same knowledge of English vocabulary. In the case of the national comparisons, it is interesting to note that the difference in results seems to reflect fairly well the existing difference in experience and teaching hours between the individual student groups.

Owing to the fact that "translating" a multiple-choice vocabulary test from one language into another creates a number of problems, the general recommendation for the use of a vocabulary test in a cross-national examination is that one should apply the test as a part of a *test battery,* not as a discrete-point test used in isolation.

There are, however, other problems connected with the use of a vocabulary test which must be taken into account when comparisons between groups of students are made. The following problems are the most obvious ones:

1. The populations can sometimes be too small for a statistical study.
2. Differences in the background of students can make all kinds of comparison difficult.
3. The test situations may not be absolutely identical.

Besides the main conclusion that university students in the Nordic countries have roughly the same knowledge of English vocabulary, the following general observations can be made:

1. Owing to the differences between languages, e.g. in respect of semantic fields, a cross-national comparison is more problematic than a national one. A national comparison, i.e. comparing results from various provinces, various cities, various schools, etc., can be most useful.
2. Like most multiple-choice tests, this test seems to possess the qualities that are desirable in a practical test according to Lado (1961:31-32): scorability, economy, and administrability.
3. This type of test would be particularly useful for measuring the vocabulary comprehension of large populations, e.g. for entrance exams for universities, for teachers' colleges, for students who are going to study abroad, etc.
4. It might also be used for testing special vocabulary, for example technical vocabulary in various branches of industry.

One major disadvantage of this type of multiple-choice vocabulary test is the fact that we are not provided with any context whatsoever. It would of course be easy to give a list of 120 sentences and to add four not quite successful synonyms as distractors to one word in each of these 120 sentences. Some part of the artificial nature of this context-free multiple-choice test would then be eliminated. The same computer program could be used for the marking.

Another disadvantage is the complexity of the distractors. By looking at the print-out of the *item analysis* we can judge if an item is too easy or too difficult. If we give the same test to various levels of students of English, one and the same item will vary a great deal with regard to discrimination. Sometimes the distractors are not sufficiently well chosen and one begins to wonder how often one is actually testing the students' ability to identify distractors rather than to identify the exact meaning of a certain word.

The multiple-choice test used is based on a word bank with fixed choices kept at the Gothenburg Computing Centre, Sweden. The underlying principle of this type of vocabulary test is that it is possible to measure the *range* of a person's vocabulary if the selection of items is related to the frequencies of the words. The item analysis can be further studied in Zettersten (1979).

The same system of measuring the vocabulary of large populations was applied to Chinese students by Gui Shichun of the Guangzhou Institute of Foreign Languages, Guangzhou, China, in 1981. The aim of this study was: (a) to test the vocabulary test itself, (b) to test the approximate vocabulary size of Chinese students at different levels, and, (c) to study the relation between vocabulary knowledge and verbal ability. One interesting result of the investigation was that vocabulary proficiency seemed to correlate highly with verbal activity. See further the *Proceedings of the International Symposium on Language Testing,* Hong Kong, 19-21 December, 1982 (Pergamon Press, 1985).

The system for testing vocabulary was also used in Finland by Christer Påhlsson at the Swedish School for Business Administration, Helsinki. See further Christer Påhlsson, "A Finnish Profile. A Report on English Vocabulary Proficiency in Nordic Countries", *Papers from the First Conference for English Studies* (ed. by Johansson-Tysdahl, 1981), pp. 355-69.

I should also like to mention another experiment which can be used for testing large populations. It is a Swedish multiple-choice vocabulary test given to foreign students from 15 different nations. The reason that I should like to discuss it briefly here is that it is an example of a cross-national comparison. This type of vocabulary test could equally well have been based on English and given to a number of students of English comprised of various nationalities.

The Swedish vocabulary test was given to a number of students of Swedish who took part in the academic summer course at Grebbestad, Sweden, organized by the Swedish Institute. The participants in the course came from 15 different countries, namely Belgium, Bulgaria, Canada, Czechoslovakia, England, the Federal Republic of Germany,

Finland, France, the German Democratic Republic, Holland, Italy, Jugoslavia, Poland, Switzerland, and the United States. In most cases the students had had between 200 and 400 hours of Swedish in their home countries. A few of the participants were themselves teachers of Swedish.

One hundred words were used in the test. The words were taken from Nils Frick – Sten Malmström, *Språkklyftan*, from 1976. In Frick-Malmström's study a corpus of approximately 700 Swedish words were investigated with regard to recognition. The 700 Swedes who took part in Frick-Malmström's study were participants in courses arranged by the National Labour Board at seven different centres in 1971, 1974, 1975. According to Frick-Malmström, people with some form of higher education were underrepresented in the investigation. At the same time, people with speech handicaps were also underrepresented. These 700 Swedes represented what could probably be considered a cross-section of the Swedish public, the average Swede, so to speak.

The 700 words chosen were up-to-date words, current in social, economic, political contexts, etc., words which would be encountered in newspapers, on radio and television broadcasts, and so on. The questions were open-ended. The test measured the passive vocabulary, and in addition to that, the use of open-ended items gave Frick and Malmström the opportunity of analysing in detail the numerous misunderstandings that occurred.

When reading the book and the reviews, I conceived the idea of testing some of the words on foreign students of Swedish. I selected 20 words from each of the following categories:

1. 0- 20 Words connected with everyday economy, such as *attestera, avi, fullmakt, kalkyl,* etc.
2. 21- 40 Value-loaded debate words, such as *absurd, fanatism, infiltrera, lojal,* etc.
3. 41- 60 Words connected with medicine, such as *desinficera, epidemi, jourhavande,* etc.
4. 61- 80 Words connected with meetings and committee life, such as *bordlägga, kandidat, kompromissa, koncept,* etc.
5. 81-100 Genuinely Swedish words, such as *arvode, behörig, idel, lekman,* etc.

From the statistics provided by Frick-Malmström, I was able to make a list of the hundred words with a figure indicating the percentage of people *not* knowing the word in question. For example, 66 % of the Swedes did not know the word *promemoria* (no. 18), 75 % did not know *infiltrera* (no. 31), and 77 % had no idea what *reaktioner* (no. 40) means. On the other hand, nobody was in any doubt as to the meaning of *gynekolog* (no. 46).

After the analysis of the results, it was easy to observe that the foreign students had their best results in categories 2 and 3, that is, value-loaded debate words and medical words. In these categories there were a great number of international words which occur in similar forms in many languages.

There are numerous sources of error in a comparative study like this, where native speakers are compared to speakers of Swedish as a foreign language. The following drawbacks may be mentioned:

1. The comparison between the *average* Swede with a *select* number of foreign students who knew a good number of international words through their mother tongue or some other language.
2. The Swedes worked with open-ended items, the foreign students had a multiple-choice test.
3. The distractors were sometimes too easy, sometimes too misleading.
4. Sometimes a distractor causes misunderstandings in one language and is rather neutral in some of the other languages.

But in spite of the existing drawbacks, my intention was to provide an example of how a cross-national study of vocabulary proficiency might be carried out.

The computer program for automatic scoring, item analysis, etc., mentioned in this chapter, is greatly suitable for distance testing. It has been used since the 1970's in Swedish academic long-distance courses in English. Swedes living abroad, either permanently or temporarily, may choose from about 10 academic subjects and within their area of choice may finish parts of or even a full first degree while living abroad. The written exams are done at the Swedish embassies and consulates abroad, written assignments are regularly sent home for correction (Uppsala University or Liber Hermods Distance Education Institute), and oral exams are taken in connection with visits to Sweden during the study period.

The same vocabulary test as was used in the Nordic survey mentioned above was given to groups of Swedish students of English in Africa and it was quite obvious that the long-distance students had better vocabulary proficiency than students studying at universities at home in Scandinavia.

The computerization can be used in an even wider context by providing pre-programmed answers to the student assignments in a distance education system. The so-called CADE system for distance education will be described in Chapter 12.

The system of computer-scoring for the survey in the Nordic countries was also used for preparing a model for the distance-testing of students at the Open University of Thailand, Sukhothaithammathirat University.

In order to get a varied picture of the means of testing large populations, I also used similar test methods with the following techniques:

1. Self-assessment with the aid of Viewdata. See further Chapter 4.
2. Self-assessment on the microcomputer (homecomputer). See also Chapter 3.
3. Testing with specific purposes (TSF), i.e. self-assessment using teletext in connection with TV-programmes. See also Chapter 5.

It is obvious that these three new technologies will add another dimension to the practice of self-assessment, providing ease, accuracy, convenience, and the possibility of repeating tests for improved performance.

A great deal of experience in the field of self-assessment has been gained within the Modern Languages Project of the Council of Europe. A study investigating various forms of guided self-assessment in language learning was prepared for the Council of Europe by Mats Oskarsson. See further M. Oskarsson (1978), *Approaches to Self-assessment in Foreign Language Learning*. It is particulary interesting to observe how *topics* and *language functions* according to the specifications in *The Threshold Level* (van Ek, 1975) can be the object of self-assessment. The following example from the model for a questionnaire (Oskarsson, p. 46) illustrates the function of inquiring about disagreement or agreement. The questionnaire should be presented in the learner's mother tongue.

1. I can ask a person if he or she is of the same opinion as
   I am   Yes   No
   Do you agree?
   Don't you think so?

This type of self-assessment of language functions in connection with the threshold level can be easily transferred to a viewdata system. The viewdata system lends itself very well to a yes/no test with a pre-programmed evaluation of the individual scores. The vocabulary test on viewdata which was described in chapter 4 is equipped with such pre-programmed pictures indicating individual results in a self-assessment situation. A similar test based on the threshold level vocabulary (1,342 words) can be constructed for viewdata, teletext, or a microcomputer. The following list of words (in principle every tenth word of the TL vocabulary) could, for example, be the basis for such a test, although one must be aware that many of these words have several meanings. See fig. 13.

1 ABOUT	26 DEAR	51 INSURANCE	76 PRICE
2 ADULT	27 DICTIONARY	52 JACKET	77 PRONOUNCE
3 AGREE	28 DINNER	53 KEEP	78 PURSE
4 AMUSEMENT	29 DO	54 LAKE	79 RAIN
5 APPLY	30 DRESS	55 LEARN	80 RED
6 ASHTRAY	31 EARLY	56 LIE	81 RETURN
7 BACK	32 END	57 LOOK	82 RIGHT
8 BATH	33 EVENING	58 LOW	83 ROUGH
9 BEDROOM	34 EXCURSION	59 MANY	84 SAME
10 BETWEEN	35 FAR	60 MEAN	85 SCISSORS
11 BLUE	36 FEEL	61 MILK	86 SELL
12 BOTH	37 FINALLY	62 MONEY	87 SHADE
13 BRING	38 FLOOR	63 MR	88 SHOE
14 BUSY	39 FOR	64 NEAR	89 SIMPLE
15 CAN	40 FREE	65 NEWSPAPER	90 SIZE
16 CARRY	41 GALE	66 NOTHING	91 SMALL
17 CHAIR	42 GIRL	67 OF	92 SOMEBODY
18 CHICKEN	43 GOVERNMENT	68 OPINION	93 SPEED
19 CLEAN	44 GROCER	69 OVER	94 STAIR
20 COAT	45 HAPPEN	70 PART	95 STILL

21 CONGRATU-LATION	46 HEART	71 PENCIL	96 STRONG
22 CORNER	47 HIGH	72 PICTURE	97 SUITCASE
23 COUNTRY	48 HORSE	73 PLANE	98 SWEET
24 CROSS	49 HURRY	74 POSSIBLE	99 TALL
25 DANGEROUS	50 INCH	75 POSTER	100 TENT

Fig. 13

The selection of material for language testing is a subject which can be debated in great detail. In order to explain the great diversity of such basic material, I have made a list of relevant material of all kinds, spoken as well as written. The following types of material may be mentioned:

Spoken:
1. Surreptitious speech. Hidden microphones. Spontaneous free conversations.
2. Live situations. Native interviewer.
3. Interview in studio. Native interviewer.
4. Summary of film. Action. Videotapes.
5. Comments on cartoons. No text.
6. Comments on a set of pictures. No text. Collages.
7. Interview. Foreign language teacher.
8. Interview. Schoolmate.
9. Retelling of story. Tape or videotapes.
10. Summary of written text.
11. Repetition of sentences. Tapes or videotapes.
12. Oral translation.

Written:
1. Diaries, etc.
2. Letters to friends.
3. Free compositions. "What did you do yesterday", "My Hobby," etc.
4. Summary of film (action). Videotape.
5. Comments on cartoons. No text.
6. Comments on a set of pictures. No text. Collages.
7. Summary of story. Tape or videotape.
8. Summary of written article.
9. Translation test.
10. Translation of specific sentences. Elicitation.
11. Repetition of sentences. Tape or videotape.
12. Dictation. Comprehension tests.

138

Spontaneity scale
Spoken:

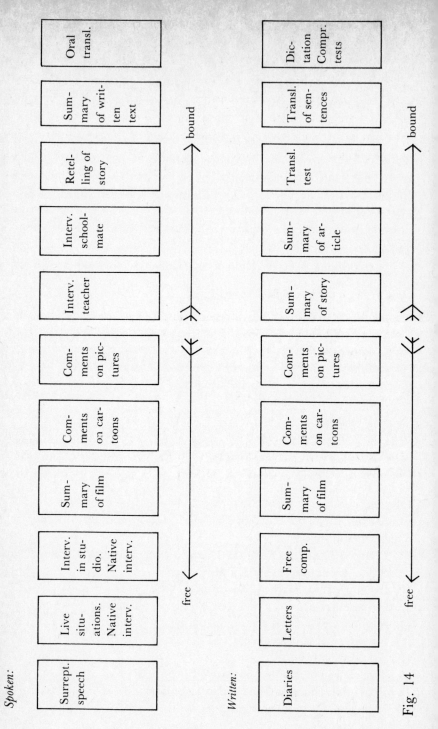

Fig. 14

The various types of material have been placed in order of spontaneity, that is, the most spontaneous category of spoken language is placed as no. 1 in the first list and diaries at the corresponding place in the second list. It is quite clear that it is sometimes debatable whether one particular category should be placed higher or lower than a neighbouring category on the list. Sometimes the material under one category can be widely different in style and degree of spontaneity. Therefore these lists can be used only as general guide-lines and as a background for comparison between individual recordings or texts.

The various categories may be placed on a kind of spontaneity scale with "free" types of speech and text to the left and "bound" types to the right, for the purpose of obtaining the most suitable material for each test situation. See Figure 14.

Chapter 11: **Sources and further reading**

Allen, J. P. B./Davies, Alan, eds. (1977), *The Edinburgh Course in Applied Linguistics*, Vol. 4: *Testing and Experimental Methods*. London: Oxford University Press.

Allen, M. J./Yen, W. M., (1979), *Introduction to Measurement Theory*. Monterey, Ca.: Brooks-Cole Publishing.

Canale, M./Swain, M. (1980), "Theoretical bases of communicative approaches to second language teaching and testing", *Applied Linguistics*, Vol. 1.1, pp. 1-47.

Carroll, Brendan J. (1980), *Testing Communicative Performance: an Interim Study*. Oxford: Pergamon Press.

Clark, John L. D., ed. (1978), *Direct Testing of Speaking Proficiency: Theory and Application: Proceedings of a Two-Day Conference*. Princeton, N. J.: Educational Testing Service.

Finocchiaro, Mary/Sako, Sydney (1980), *Foreign Language Testing: a Practical Approach*. New York: Regents Publishing.

Frick, N./Malmström, S. (1976), *Språkklyftan*. Kristianstad: Tidens förlag.

Frith, James R., ed. (1980), *Measuring Spoken Language Proficiency*. Washington, DC: Georgetown University Press.

Harrison, Andrew (1983), *A Language Testing Handbook*. Basingstoke: Macmillan Education.

Hatch, E./Farhady, H. (1982), *Research Design and Statistics for Applied Linguistics*. Rowley, Mass.: Newbury House.

Heaton, J. B., ed. (1982), *Language Testing*. Oxford: Modern English Publications.

Johansson, S./Tysdahl, B. J. (1981), *Papers from the First Conference for English Studies*, Oslo, 17-19 September, 1980.

Jones, R. L./Spolsky, B., eds. (1975), *Testing Language Proficiency*. Washington, DC: Center for Applied Linguistics.

Lewis, E. G./Massad, C. E. (1975), *The Teaching of English as a Foreign Language in Ten Countries*. Stockholm: Almqvist & Wiksell.

Oller, J. W., Jr. (1979), *Language Tests at School: a Pragmatic Approach*. London: Longman.

Oller, J. W., Jr., ed. (1981), *Issues in Language Testing Research*. Rowley, Mass.: Newbury House.

Oller, J. W., Jr./Perkins, K., eds. (1980), *Research in Language Testing*. Rowley, Mass.: Newbury House.

Oskarsson, Mats (1980), *Approaches to Self-Assessment in Foreign Language Learning*. Prepared for the Council of Europe by Mats Oskarsson. New ed. Oxford, New York: Pergamon Press for and on behalf of the Council of Europe Modern Languages Project.

Proceedings of the International Symposium on Language Testing, Hong Kong, 19-21 December, 1982. Oxford: Pergamon Press (1985).

Spolsky, Bernard, ed. (1978), *Approaches to Language Testing*. Washington, DC: Center for Applied Linguistics.

Spolsky, Bernard, ed. (1979), *Some Major Tests*. Washington, DC: Center for Applied Linguistics.

Chapter 12

Distance education.
The future of self-education.
Continuing education

Various references to distance education have been made in some of the previous chapters. Both *Viewdata* (chapter 4) and *Teletext* (chapter 5) are particularly important to mention as future aids in distance education. The importance of certain new techniques for language testing in distance education programs was also referred to in chapter 11.

In his *Recent Research into Distance Education* (1982), p. 3, B. Holmberg states that during the 1970's distance education meant "the various forms of study at all levels which are not under the continuous, immediate supervision of tutors present with their students in lecture rooms or on the same premises, but which, nevertheless, benefit from the planning, guidance and tuition of a tutorial organisation."

However, as Holmberg also points out (p. 4), there seem to be at least two different schools of thought regarding distance education. According to Holmberg: "one stressing individual study and individual, non-contiguous tutoring on the basis of course materials produced for large groups of students, the other aiming at parallelism with resident study and usually including class or group teaching face-to-face as a regular element." An overview of tendencies and innovations at the beginning of the 1980's can be obtained from Daniel, J.S., *et al.* (1982), *Learning at a Distance. A World Perspective.* It is obvious that modern advances in communications technology have changed the possibilities and the potential of distance education in the future.

Mainframe computers have been used for several years in distance education. Most of the systems have been off-line systems used for marking tests, reporting results and making statistical analyses. One system is called CADE (=Computer Assisted Distance Education) developed at Liber-Hermods, Malmö, Sweden, by John A. Bååth and N.O. Månsson in the 1970's. In this system the students' assignments are scanned by an optical reader and the relevant comments are selected by the computer according to the profile of the results. See Bååth – Månsson (1977) *CADE – A System for Computer-Assisted Distance Education*. Another similar system is called RSVP, developed at Dade Community College, Miami. See K. Anandam (1976), *RSVP. A Guide for Implementia*.

In a distance test I produced myself, the students received a computer-generated proficiency profile with a description of their individual level in five different sectors of language proficiency: (1) vocabulary, (2) oral production, (3) listening comprehension, (4) pronunciation, (5) written production.

These descriptions of proficiency levels, which will be given below, could also be used in various other distance testing contexts, for example, employment tests for business companies.

Description of Proficiency Levels (10-0)

	1.	2.	3.	4.	5.
	Vocabulary	Oral Production	Listening Comprehension	Pronunciation	Written Production
10	The vocabulary is extremely large and varied and sufficiently good to cope with extremely complicated topics.	Completely correct dialect-free oral production with very advanced vocabulary. Adequate content matter.	Maximum listening comprehension.	Like a native R.P. speaker.	Completely correct written production with highly qualified vocabulary. Adequate content matter.

9	The vocabulary is very large and varied and sufficiently good to cope with very complicated topics.	Completely correct dialect-free oral production with advanced vocabulary. Adequate content matter.	Nearly maximum listening comprehension.	Practically like a native R.P. speaker.	Completely correct written production with qualified vocabulary. Adequate content matter.
8	The vocabulary is large and varied and sufficiently good to cope with complicated topics.	Very good dialect-free oral production with very good vocabulary. Adequate content matter.	Very good listening comprehension.	Very good dialect-free pronunciation.	Nearly completely correct written production with good vocabulary. Adequate content matter.
7	The vocabulary is rather large and varied and sufficiently good to cope with everyday situations.	Good dialect-free oral production with good vocabulary. The content matter tolerably adequate.	Good listening comprehension.	Good dialect-free pronunciation. Certain interference from mother tongue.	Tolerably correct written production with good vocabulary. The content matter tolerably adequate.
6	The vocabulary is satisfactory for everyday situations. In more specific, professional contexts the vocabulary is not sufficient.	Satisfactory oral production with satisfactory vocabulary. The content matter tolerably adequate.	Satisfactory listening comprehension.	Satisfactory pronunciation. The speaker can make himself clearly understood but there is some interference from mother tongue in pronunciation and intonation.	Tolerably correct written production with satisfactory vocabulary. The content matter tolerably adequate.

5	The vocabulary is fairly satisfactory for general contexts and everyday situations. In more specific professional contexts the vocabulary is quite insufficient.	Fairly satisfactory oral production with fairly satisfactory vocabulary. The content matter not adequate in all respects.	Fairly satisfactory listening comprehension.	Fairly satisfactory pronunciation. The speaker can make himself understood well, but there is clear interference from the mother tongue in pronunciation and intonation.	The written production is not correct in all respects, but the vocabulary is fairly satisfactory. The content matter is not quite adequate.
4	The vocabulary is not quite satisfactory. It may be sufficient for simple conversation but it is too narrow for contexts beyond everyday conversation.	Not quite satisfactory oral production. Clear weaknesses in vocabulary and too many gaps in the content matter.	Not quite satisfactory listening comprehension.	Not quite satisfactory pronunciation. The speaker can make himself understood but there is clear interference from mother-tongue in pronunciation and intonation.	Not quite satisfactory written production. Too many inadequacies both in vocabulary and content matter.
3	The vocabulary unsatisfactory. Even for simple tasks the vocabulary is too small.	Clear deficiencies in the oral production. Vocabulary too small and the content matter quite unsatisfactory.	Clear deficiencies in listening comprehension.	Clear deficiencies in pronunciation. The basic sound formation must be greatly improved on. Very marked interference from mother tongue.	Clear deficiencies in written production. The vocabulary too small and the content matter inadequate.

2	The vocabulary is most unsatisfactory.	Very great deficiencies in the oral production. The vocabulary is very small. The content matter most inadequate.	Very great deficiencies in listening comprehension.	Very great deficiencies in the pronunciation of English words. Many misconceptions are caused by errors.	Very great deficiencies in the written production. The vocabulary is very small. The content matter highly inadequate.
1	The vocabulary is extremely small.	Hardly any ability to produce spoken English.	Hardly any ability to comprehend spoken English.	Hardly any ability to pronounce English words.	Hardy any ability to produce written English.
0	Hardly any vocabulary at all.	No ability to produce spoken English.	No ability to comprehend spoken English.	No ability to pronounce English.	No ability to produce written English.

In more recent years it has proved possible to run similar systems on a microcomputer. A system called MAIL was, for example, developed at the National Extension College, Cambridge, England, by which teachers can produce their own comment files for their test material. The system generates detailed personal letters to the home-based students. The MAIL system, which runs on a BBC microcomputer, can also be linked to an already existing computer system in a school or distance-education institute. See further R. Freeman (1984), "MAIL: Micro-Aided Learning", *Computers and Education*, 8:1, pp. 203-8.

It is also important to mention on-line use of computers, for example instructional work at computer terminals in study centres at the Open University in England.

One may look at the use of communications technology for distance education in two ways. The first type is the *live/transmitted computing*, for example radio and television programmes sent at specific times. Richard Hooper, in his article, "The Computer as a Medium for Distance Education," *World Yearbook of Education 1982/83. Computers and Education* (ed. by J. Megarry, *et al.*, 1983), recognizes three types of computing in the live/ transmitted mode:

1. two-way computer-assisted learning in tutorial and/or simulation style.
2. one-way information retrieval.
3. computer-assisted live teaching.

The PLATO system is an excellent example of a two-way CAL system. Another example is Viewdata, for instance, the British Prestel system. Prestel can be used for home education at various stages. Cf. for example the article by P. Fidely – L. Yaun, "Prestel and home education for young children", *Computers and Education*, 8:1 (1984), pp. 209-11. In connection with language training, literacy programs on Prestel should be particularly mentioned here. Attention is drawn in the above-mentioned article to a phonic program practising initial sounds for very young children.

Under the second type of computing for distance learning, namely one-way information retrieval, the use of teletext should be considered. As for computer assisted live teaching, the Open University system CYCLOPS is undoubtedly the best known. CYCLOPS is an audio-visual system based on a television set, audio cassettes and a micro-computer. The visual information or pictures, as well as the audio information, are recorded on the stereo cassette. Pictures from a light pen can be transmitted between tutors and students via the telephone line. The CYCLOPS system represents both the live/ transmitted and the recorded/ local medium according to Hooper's article. All the software programs produced for microcomputers (personal computers) also represent the recorded/ local type. As was mentioned in chapter 4, all kinds of telesoftware whereby computer programs can be downloaded via viewdata (such as Prestel) and teletext (such as Ceefax) to personal computers, will become increasingly important for distance learners in the future.

Modern technology is currently capable of delivering learning systems so much quicker and with such greater accuracy than before and over greater distances as well, that it may be justified to refer to some of the varieties of distance learning in the wider context of self-learning. Particularly since certain of the exercises produced with the aid of new technologies are self-generating and can be modelled according to the user's own capability and level of progress, it is appropriate to characterize the process as self-learning. However, as is pointed out by Henry

Holec in *Autonomy and Foreign Language Learning* (1980), p. 5, "the extent to which a teacher is physically present is not a good standard to judge the extent to which learning is self-directed: whether a teacher is present or not as learning proceeds, it is principally the role of the learner which is the determining factor of self-directed learning." It is very likely that if some of the new technologies take into account the specific nature and needs of each individual more comprehensively than earlier methods, we shall be able to characterize the process as individualization and self-education with greater justification.

Chapter 12: Sources and further reading

Bates, T. (1982), "Trends in the Use of Audio-Visual Media in Distance Education Systems", in J.S. Daniel *et al. Learning at a Distance*, pp. 8-15.

Bramer, M. (1980), "Using computers in distance education: The first ten years of the British Open University", *Computers and Education* 4, pp. 293-301.

Bååth, J.A. (1982), "Experimental Research on Computer-Assisted Distance Education", in J.S. Daniel *et al.* (eds.) *Learning at a Distance*, pp. 303-305.

Bååth, J./ Månsson, N.-O. (1977), *CADE – A System for Computer-Assisted Distance Education*. Malmö: Hermods skola.

Daniel, J.S./ Stroud, M.A./ Thompson, J.R., ed. (1982), *Learning at a Distance. A World Perspective*. Edmonton: Athabasca University/ International Council for Correspondence Education.

D'Antoni, S.G. (1982), "Videodisc and Videotex: New Media for Distance Education", in J.S. Daniel et al. (eds.) *Learning at a Distance*, pp. 287-290.

Distance Teaching by Cyclops: An Evaluation of the O.Us Telewriting Systems (1982), *JET Paper* No. 202. Milton Keynes: The Open University.

Holec, H. (1980), *Autonomy and Foreign Language Learning*. Strasbourg: Council of Europe.

Holmberg, B. (1981), *Status and Trends of Distance Education*. London: Kogan Page.

Holmberg, B. (1982), *Recent Research into Distance Education*. Hagen: FernUniversität.

Hooper, R. (1983), "The computer as a medium for distance education", in J. Megarry *et al.* (1983).*World Yearbook of Education 1982/83*, pp. 103-108.

Megarry, J., *et al.* (1983), *World Yearbook of Education 1982/83: Computers and Education*. London: Kogan Page.

OLS Newsletter. Newsletter about Open Learning Systems. Sponsored by the Council for Educational Technology and the Scottish Council for Educational Technology. Southampton.

Open Learning. CET Information Sheet no. 5 (March 1984). London: Council for Educational Technology.

Ruggles, R.H. *et al.* (1982), *Learning at a Distance and the New Technology*. Vancouver: Educational Research Institute of British Columbia.

Chapter 13

A new super-media model of language learning.
Flexible combinations of different
media (media-mix)

So-called *multi-media courses* have been known for a long time, although the variety of media involved has not always been very impressive. Sometimes a radio or TV programme, a textbook and some audio-tapes have constituted a "package" which may have been termed a multi-media course. Some of the language courses on the market have, on the other hand, been excellent, and have helped to make language learning much more authentic and worthwhile.

In chapter 9, which dealt with the use of authentic material, I drew attention to a special issue of the *British Journal of Language Teaching*, Vol. XVIII, 2-3 (1980), dealing with "The use of broadcast material in language teaching", in which some articles discussed multi-media systems. One article by P.J. Downes on "A Multi-media Approach to Language Teaching: Variations on a Theme", discussed French topics like "Ordering drinks and snacks in a café". The following components were recommended by Downes:

1. Overhead projector transparency.
2. Filmstrip and tape-recording.
3. Cassette recording of conversations.
4. Pupil's book.
5. Television scenes.
6. Tape-recorded listening comprehension exercises.
7. Colour slides of café scenes.

Multi-media courses like these became extremely popular in many countries during the 1970's. One of the most complex and successful ones was *"Follow Me"*, which was a cooperative work, involving several institutions both in Great Britain and the Federal Republic of Germany. The course components of *"Follow Me"* were:

1. Television
2. Radio.
3. Self-study materials (2 books, 2 audio-cassettes).
4. Course materials.
5. Teacher's materials (1 handbook, 2 audio cassettes).

This multi-media course design was based on the work of the Council of Europe Modern Languages Project and thus on a functional/ notional approach. As was pointed out by Sheila Innes in an article called "The Development of BBC Involvement in Multi-media Language Programmes" in the above-mentioned issue of the *British Journal of Language Teaching*, p. 167, "the most effective multi-media courses are not necessarily those which make use of the largest number of components." Sheila Innes makes it clear that it is essential to create a course with the user very much in mind. She suggests the following check-list of questions for such multi-media courses.

1. Is the learning designed consciously to diminish anxiety?
2. Is there as little reliance as possible on short-term memory?
3. Is the learning based on activity by the learner?
4. Can the learner himself control the pace at which he works?
5. Is the learner likely to achieve success with his learning at every stage?
6. Can the learner find out whether he has learnt correctly?
7. Is the material to be learnt interesting and stimulating?
8. Does it take into account the adult learner's existing experience?
9. Is he likely to accept the learning as relevant to his own interests?
10. Are opportunities for constant practice built in?
11. Can learners participate in learning with others?

The same check-list of questions can be used in another area of multi-media courses, namely those based on the use of a microcomputer, e.g. the so-called "CAL packages", which belong to the 1980's. One example is a package called "APFELDEUTSCH" to be used on the Apple computer. The package consists of a coursebook, *Grundkurs Deutsch*

(München, 1980), a workbook, six audiotapes, and nine computer disks. Similar packages can be built up around any type of writing course material for second language learners. The new multi-media courses including microcomputer exercises as a component, are not necessarily parallel to the ones based on radio or TV. The radio and TV courses were usually based on a radio or TV series with coursebooks and workbooks and tapes as support material. The micro-computer courses usually have a written language course as the central component and the micro exercises serve as support material. The focus in the first case is thus the radio or TV broadcast with a view to provide authentic situations or language functions. The task of the modern language teacher is to bring these two conceptions together and to create something new and better than the two original models. The task of those interested in modern technologies in language learning is to link the existing technologies, such as TV, with some of the more recent ones and to build up a *super-media model for language learning*.

A step in this direction is the use of a *component television system*, which may consist of a monitor, with various input and output jacks for linking up with video, videodisc players, microcomputers, cable television, etc. Cf. also the broadband communication system called BIG-FON, presented in chapter 10.

We have already discussed in chapters 3-12 how various technologies may be utilized in education in general and in language learning in particular. The examples given were usually descriptions of how one new technology could be used to reinforce certain fixed language skills. In order to reach further and to add more variety to the learning process, a more advanced system of combining several technologies must be created. The aim should be to move beyond drills and practices including as much interaction as possible and increasing the availability of specialized data-bases.

The models of such broad learning systems may be achieved by looking at certain advanced *business systems,* which have been built up in the form of *networks* in business companies. Local area networks (=LANS), in contrast to public and private telephone networks are computer-based systems which are formed by a series of terminals via a coaxial or optical fibre circuit. According to D. Longley – M. Shain (1982), *Dictionary of Information Technology,* p. 42, there are several distinct services that a LAN should perform, such as "access to mainframes videotex, desk-top computing, internal memory and paging functions such as manager's diary, conference planning, word processing, access to telex and facsimile, electronic mail, image generation, message handling and voice transmission."

The new cable systems based on coaxial or optical fibres will be able to provide many of the new telecommunication-based services to home as well as to work. With the new high-capacity datalinks joining homes and business companies, the planning of continuing education will be much more rewarding.

Since business companies and large organizations are likely to be better and better supplied with electronic equipment, there is a greater chance for the language training divisions of such companies, rather than for schools and individuals, to have access to many varieties of language learning techniques. It is also likely that new developments in methodology will be quicker and better in business companies. It is therefore important to encourage research and experimentation in companies as well as to link technical progress at work with self-study at home and with basic education, such as computer literacy, at school. If we accept that a technological society is inevitable or necessary for economic growth, it would probably be a wise investment to concentrate our efforts upon making computer literacy universal from primary school through secondary school, and in job-specific education, continuing education and self-study.

Foreign language learning should of course have a share in such a universal training system. Any society or any government will find it increasingly necessary to train and retrain as many people as possible in the use of modern technology in education. If this is not done, there will always be the fear that we shall create a society consisting of two layers, one computer-literate and one computer-illiterate group. If universal training is not undertaken in a country, that particular country runs the risk of losing touch with technical developments in the rest of the world. The gap between technological countries and non-technological countries will then widen, just as the gap between the computer-literate and the computer-illiterate will be greater in the future.

The technological evolution has, indeed, been rapid and revolutionary. One would therefore hope that the new technologies will be applied to modern theories of language learning within the near future.

151

In Færch/Haastrup/Phillipson (1984), *Learner Language and Language Learning*, a model is presented which sees foreign language learning as a cognitive process of *hypothesis formation* and *hypothesis testing*, supplemented by processes of *automatization* and *consciousness raising* (see pp. 185-206).

A major task for software writers in the 1980's will be to devote more interest than before to programs which may facilitate the various processes of language learning like the ones discussed by Færch/Haastrup/Phillipson.

With combinations of microcomputers, including audio units, video, videodiscs, viewdata, teletext, etc., the possibilities of further improvements in the techniques of second language learning seem excellent. Only one point should be particularly observed, namely the question of tools for conversational management. In most exercises available on the market, based on only one of the technologies, there is no attempt to help the users to practice communication with native speakers. Some excellent simulations can be given with the aid of videodisc programs and some tools for conversational management are provided through all the examples of *combinatory acquisition* given, for example, in chapters 6 and 7. The philosophy behind my use of the term *combinatory acquisition* is that when learners become absorbed in a specific problem-solving activity, such as producing a videofilm with only nominal supervision, they lose their inhibitions concerning the target language. This can be accomplished in a variety of ways, some of which are very simple. One simple way of using the idea of combinatory acquisition is to use the target language consistently in all communication about and around the microcomputer or whatever technological aid is being used in a study situation where an instructor is involved. In the case of individual users of these learning systems, the possibility of actually training communication beyond simulation is of course much more restricted.

This fact leads us back to the important statement that the new machines cannot replace a native speaker or a good foreign language teacher and they are not meant to do so. They should be regarded as extremely useful complements to a teacher, and to many foreign language learners they are and will be regarded as completely indispensible tools.

What should the future of foreign language learning aim at? That it

152

will be greatly enhanced by more and more technologies seems to me to be clear, and I am supported by many other people in my assumption. To discuss the question of *what the future of language learning will look like* seems, however, to be futile, since such rapid changes have already taken place in the 70's and 80's and many more are likely to come quite suddenly. I have already mentioned the fact that we shall be expecting a fifth generation of computers, and new ways of telecommunications through satellites and optical fibres will increase the technical possibilities of gaining access to all kinds of educational programs. The production of educational programs has, as has been explained previously in this book, not kept pace with the technological leaps, a fact which makes predictions about the future even more complicated and uncertain. It is therefore appropriate to discuss the aim of foreign language learning in the future. My view is that software producers and individual programmers should bear in mind two advantages that the microcomputers have and which make them important as complementary tools in any language learning system. Firstly they are *individualizing*. The programs may be suited so well to the individual that we may sometimes justifiably characterize such programs as a form of tailor-made instruction. Secondly, they are *interactive*. The learning process based on the use of a microcomputer or some of the other new technologies is an active process, which is not true of book-based or TV-based education or even necessarily of teacher-based training.

James W. Johnson in his article "Education and the New Technology: A Force of History", *Educational Technology*, October (1981), p. 18, has expressed similar ideas in the following manner: "The new technology is *demassed;* videodisc and videotex let you choose your own sources, news and other information, and computing lets you do these things interactively in your own home."

Johnson also points out that the computer gives all the other technological devices *intelligence*.

Alfred Bork, who is very critical of the quality of the present computer-based learning material, also explains why "the computer is destined to be an important factor in human learning at all levels with all types of people." In an article, "Computers and the future education", *Computers and Education*, Vol. 8:1 (1984), p. 2, he gives the following explanation: "Fundamentally the major factor is *Interaction.*"

Finally, I would like to emphasize that the new technologies represent a potential watershed in language education, if only we have the receptivity and the imagination to use them properly. We should not lose sight of the ultimate goal of language education which is to achieve inter-human communication and cross-cultural understanding. There is no reason why technology cannot be employed to serve humanist goals and there is no reason that it should not be so encouraged. The great impact of the new technologies on our daily lives is an undeniable fact, the human use of the new technologies is the challenge to which we as educators must respond.

Chapter 14
Summing up

The implications, consequences and considerations connected with the use of the new technologies are many indeed. This summary reflects my personal view of ways in which the new technologies may prove to be useful for individual learners, for schools and other educational establishments, for business companies and large organizations, and for society in general. I shall summarize my viewpoints one by one and without particular priority implied by the order in which they are presented. For the sake of convenience and reference, I shall refer to the pertinent chapters in the book in which fuller accounts are to be found.

1. Exercises using new technologies should be regarded as complements or as auxiliary aids for language teachers, and not as a replacement for their role. See chapter 1. New technologies will relieve language teachers of tedious or repetitive tasks and thereby enable them to concentrate to a greater degree on the communicative aspects of language teaching. See chapter 2.

2. I do not foresee any dramatic innovation in the field of methodology that will make the learning of languages appreciably faster in the future. The greater leaps ahead will undoubtedly come about through the appropriate use of new technologies in language learning. See chapter 1.

3. One of the key issues in second language learning is the balance between accuracy and fluency. The existence of new technologies will facilitate the improvement of both accuracy and fluency at every level of application. See chapter 2.

4. We are currently dealing with the fourth and fifth generations of computers. The corresponding software production in language training, on the other hand, may be characterized as the first generation of language learning programs. Software writers have been slow to produce adequate courseware. See chapter 3.

5. The microcomputer is the key instrument in the development of new technologies in language learning in the 1980's, both as a self-supporting aid and as a link to other media and other systems. It is important to emphasize that it is *interactive* and that it is greatly *individualized*. See chapters 3 and 13.

6. There are many ways in which microcomputers can be enhanced, for example, with the aid of audio devices, touch screens, sound generators, speech synthesis, and various types of software. See chapters 3 and 4.

7. Viewdata is an interactive videotex system, which can be used for learning grammar and vocabulary, as well as for language testing. The access to large databases, dictionaries, etc., will open up new possibilities for home-users, schools and business companies. See chapter 4.

8. Teletext is a non-interactive videotex system. For introducing radio and TV programmes, for providing glossaries, teleflashes, tests and exercises in distance education, teletext is a most useful aid. See chapters 4 and 12.

9. Video programmes were primarily used by language teachers in the 1970's as authentic illustrations of life-like situations. However, video can also be used to practise language functions. See chapter 6.

10. The videodisc will increasingly be used in the future as an instructional tool in education. Since film, sound, text, still pictures, graphics, etc., can be stored with random access, we have at our disposal an extremely flexible system. See chapter 6.

11. Since both microcomputers and video-machines will be increasingly available, microcomputer/video interface is particularly attractive. See chapter 6.

12. The technique of language training which I have called *combinatory acquisition* is implemented when learners become absorbed in a specific problem-solving activity and lose their inhibitions concerning the target language. This can be exemplified by the use of role-playing, simulation, games, drama and other similar techniques, while recording the activities on video. See chapter 7.

13. Artificial intelligence, synthetic speech and robots have very broad educational application and far-reaching consequences for language learning and for learning in general. See chapter 8.

14. Authentic material in the form of film and TV has been used by language teachers for a number of years already. The need for more material and more authentic material in the future will probably be satisfied quite easily with the expansion of optical fibre cables and the increased use of TV satellites. See chapter 9.

15. The telephone as an aid in language training has been used quite extensively, and its value has proved to be great. Audio, video and computer-based teleconferencing are all useful for practising communication. In this context satellite technology opens up many interesting perspectives. See chapter 10.

16. Language testing with the aid of computers has been practised for a considerable time. For testing large populations it is important to emphasize the use of microcomputers, viewdata, and teletext. See chapter 11.

17. There are three types of computing to be considered in distance education:

A. two-way computer-assisted learning, for example, the PLATO system or viewdata.
B. one-way information retrieval, for example, teletext.

C. computer-assisted live teaching, for example, the Open University system CYCLOPS in England. See chapter 12.

18. Multi-media courses will continue to be popular. Language learning systems may ultimately contain so many new technologies that it will be justifiable to call them super-media models of language learning. Such systems, whether they are built up in a school or a business company, can be operated with the aid of the microcomputer. See chapter 13.

19. Language learning should preferably be carried out as an organic system where the new technologies are components of the system. The aim should be to train most language skills integratively. In schools and companies language training could be organized as a station system with constant access to databases and a bank of authentic video and videodisc programs as well as relevant computer software.

20. The individual learner would then also have increasingly greater access to the same external service, for example, being able to download programs through viewdata and teletext. If maximum access to new technologies cannot be attained by every individual language learner, then a microcomputer and a video machine will, at least, constitute a most effective start.

Appendix

An authoring system for grammar exercises

The authoring system described in this appendix was developed by Mats Jacobson and myself for the Swedish microcomputer ABC 80 to be used primarily in schools by language teachers. The program was written in BASIC for teachers who had not necessarily any previous knowledge of computer programming. The programs can also be used on ABC 800, 802 and 806.

The system consists of two main parts, one program to be used by the teachers for making their own grammar lessons, and one for the students taking the exercises. The system can be used for any language with an alphabetical script. In this particular case, Swedish is the mother tongue and English the target language.

The following description shows step by step how the program is built up. Two diskettes are always used in the system: one for the *basic program* (or *lesson generator*) and one for the *data*, i.e. the various exercises and comments specific for each lesson.

We start the program by printing the command: "RUN AUTHOR". Then the following menu is shown:

```
LGENERATOR - Main menu

          What do you want to do?


     1. Edit the lesson menu

     2. Edit lessons

     3. Diskette service

     4. Take a lesson

     5. Exit


        Select a number >
```

fig. 1

First the diskette must be initiated. In order to do so, we must select alternative 3 in the main menu, which leads us to *Diskette service:*

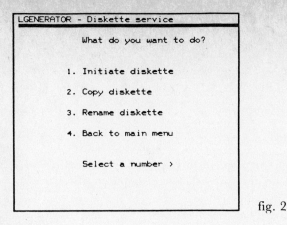

```
LGENERATOR - Diskette service

          What do you want to do?


     1. Initiate diskette

     2. Copy diskette

     3. Rename diskette

     4. Back to main menu


          Select a number >
```

fig. 2

We now choose 1 (Initiate diskette) and this diskette is ready to be used as a *data diskette* for this program. It consists of eight empty lessons. We then return to the main menu by pressing alt. 4.

Our next step is to "create a lesson", which means that we give it a number and a title. This title corresponds to a place in the lesson menu that the student will see. We now select 1 in the main menu (1. Edit the lesson menu):

```
LGENERATOR - Edit lesson menu

          What do you want to do?


     1. Create lessons

     2. Delete lessons

     3. Edit lesson titles

     4. Back to main menu


          Select a number >
```

fig. 3

We select 1 here, too, (Create lessons) and the following picture comes up:

160

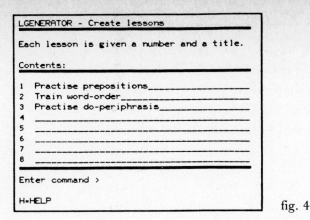

```
LGENERATOR - Create lessons

Each lesson is given a number and a title.

Contents:

1   Practise prepositions_____
2   Train word-order_____
3   Practise do-periphrasis_____
4   _____
5   _____
6   _____
7   _____
8   _____

Enter command >

H=HELP
```

fig. 4

We can see eight lines, either empty or used, as well as the numbers 1-8. On these lines the titles of the lessons are to be written in. Since line 4 is empty we can create a lesson having this number. We indicate this by typing in "4" as a command. We then insert the new title on the appropriate line. We press "RETURN" and then the command "Exit" (=E) to return to the menu (Edit lesson menu). The space for our new lesson is now cleared and ready to use, which means that we can start writing in texts and questions (tasks). We return to the main menu by selecting 4. We press 2 (Edit lessons) in the main menu and get the following picture:

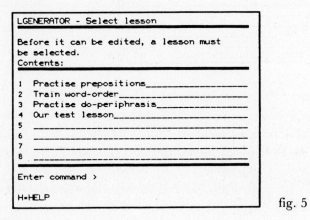

```
LGENERATOR - Select lesson

Before it can be edited, a lesson must
be selected.
Contents:

1   Practise prepositions_____
2   Train word-order_____
3   Practise do-periphrasis_____
4   Our test lesson_____
5   _____
6   _____
7   _____
8   _____

Enter command >

H=HELP
```

fig. 5

First we must indicate which lesson we want to edit (=4). After the lesson has been selected, the following picture is shown:

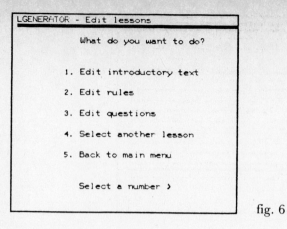

fig. 6

We are now ready to insert the introductory text (i.e. those pages that are shown as an introduction at the beginning of a lesson). We can do this after selecting 1 (Edit introductory text). Then the following picture will be shown:

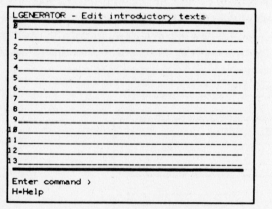

fig. 7

Every page contains 14 lines, numbered 0-13. The line number must be written in at the beginning of each line. Words are added or deleted by the commands "+" and "−" respectively. After writing, for example, "9" and pressing "RETURN", we are ready to insert the relevant text on this line. We shall now insert the following text:

162

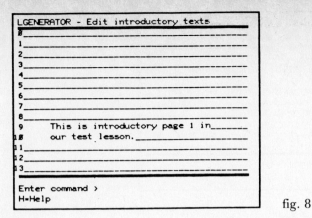

```
LGENERATOR - Edit introductory texts
0_____
1_____
2_____
3_____
4_____
5_____
6_____
7_____
8_____
9      This is introductory page 1 in_____
10     our test lesson._____
11_____
12_____
13_____

Enter command >
H=Help
```
fig. 8

When the text on this line (and line 10) has been completed, we press
"RETURN" and the program is ready to receive commands again. We then
press E for returning to the menu (Edit lessons). A grammar rule, which the
student may need when solving a particular grammar problem, can also be
inserted in the same way as the introductory text.

We now start writing in the relevant grammar task. We press 3 for editing
questions (tasks). The following picture is shown:

```
LGENERATOR - Edit questions

Question number: 1/1

Swedish sentence:
1_____
English sentence:
2_____
3Guidance: _____
4Answers : _____
Feedback:
5_____
6_____

Enter command >

H=HELP
```
fig. 9

As is seen here, every line has a number, and by writing one of these numbers,
we indicate that we want to edit the corresponding line. We thus insert a
grammar task here, for example, the following:

```
┌─────────────────────────────────────────────┐
│ LGENERATOR - Edit questions                 │
│ ═══════════════════════════════════════════ │
│ Question number: 1/1                        │
│ ═══════════════════════════════════════════ │
│ Swedish sentence:                           │
│ 1Någon hade slagit till mig medan jag sov.  │
│  English sentence:                          │
│ 2Someone had ........ me while I slept.___  │
│ 3Guidance: att slå till = to strike_____   │
│ 4Answers : struck_____       │
│  Feedback:                                  │
│ 5_____       │
│ 6_____       │
│ ═══════════════════════════════════════════ │
│ Enter command >                             │
│ ───────────────────────────────────────     │
│ H=HELP                                      │
└─────────────────────────────────────────────┘
```

fig. 10

If some additional guidance for solving the task is necessary, line 3 can be used. There is also space for a special comment in case the student answers wrongly (Feedback).

Summary of what we have done so far:

1. We initiated a diskette, so that it could be used as a *data diskette* for this program.
2. We created a lesson and gave it a title (name).
3. We typed in the introductory text after which a grammar rule could be inserted.
4. Finally we inserted a specimen task with Guidance and Answer.

We are now ready to take the lesson we have made. We therefore return to the main menu and select 4 (Take a lesson). Then the following picture is shown:

```
┌─────────────────────────────────────────────┐
│ TESTDISKETTE - Lesson menu                  │
│                                             │
│         What do you want to do?             │
│                                             │
│                                             │
│      1. Practise prepositions               │
│      2. Train word-order                    │
│      3. Practise do-periphrasis             │
│      4. Our test lesson                      │
│      5.                                      │
│      6.                                      │
│      7.                                      │
│      8.                                      │
│      9. Exit                                 │
│                                             │
│                                             │
│         Select a number >                   │
│                                             │
└─────────────────────────────────────────────┘
```

fig. 11

Only titles of lessons created can now be seen on the screen. Number 4 is selected:

This is introductory page 1 in
our test lesson

Press RETURN

fig. 12

The introductory page is now shown. The next step is a page showing the relevant grammar rule. After that comes the grammar task.

The various stages in the structure of a lesson are shown below:

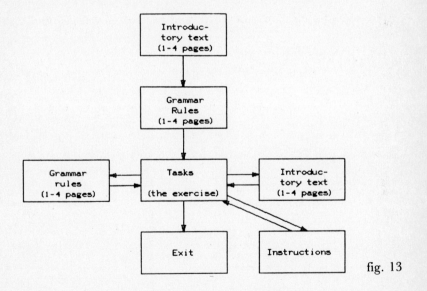

fig. 13

The various tasks recur in random order in the program. Only those tasks that were answered wrongly will be shown a second time.

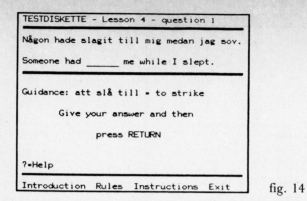

fig. 14

After having given the answer to question 1, the student is told if the answer was right or wrong. If the answer was wrong, a comment or piece of advice (FEEDBACK) is given.

List of useful terminology

ACR = Audio Cassette Recorder.

ADP = Automatic Data Processing.

AI = Artificial Intelligence. The capability of a machine to perform some of the functions of human intelligence, including learning, reasoning, self-correction and adaptation.

ASCII = American Standard Code for Information Interchange. Each character on the keyboard is assigned a unique ASCII code number in order that the computer may distinguish between them.

ATR = Audio Tape Recorder.

Authoring Language = High-level language that permits the user to program without having extensive knowledge of a computer language.

Authoring System = Special software designed for writing CAI lessons. A course authoring system automatically provides packaging and formatting for whatever lesson is written by the lesson author.

BASIC = Beginner's All-Purpose Symbolic Instruction Code. The most commonly used microcomputer programming language.

Bit = Binary Digit. The smallest unit of digital information.

Bug = A logical error in a program. (See also "Debug").

Byte = The number of bits (usually eight) required to store one character of text.

CAI = Computer-Assisted Instruction.

CAL = Computer-Assisted Learning.

CALI = Computer-Assisted Language Instruction.

CALL = Computer-Assisted Language Learning.

CAT = Computer-Assisted Teaching.

CBL = Computer Based Learning.

Chip = A small, flat piece of silicon on which electronic circuits are etched.

Compiler = A computer language translator which can translate a program into machine code and store it for later retrieval.

Computer Literacy = General skills and knowledge for the purpose of operating computers.

Courseware = A set of lessons developed for use with a computer.

CP/M = An operating system available on various microcomputers.

Database = An extensive collection of related data.

Debug = To find and to correct a logical error in a computer program.

Dialects = Variant versions of the same computer language.

EPROM = Erasable Programmable Read Only Memory. A type of ROM that can be programmed by the user, and which can be erased and reprogrammed. Compare: PROM.

Floppy Disk = A thin, round, flexible disk which is used for storage of microcomputer programs and data. The data is accessible via a Floppy Disk Drive.

Flow chart = A chart showing the actions underlying a program.

Hardware = The collection of physical devices that make up a computer system. Also known as Computer Hardware.

High-Level Languages = Languages that enable the user to employ English-like commands, rather than machine code, to communicate with the central processing unit. BASIC, COBOL, LOGO and FORTRAN are commonly used High-Level Languages.

Hz = Hertz, the frequency per second of an electrical signal.

Input = Information entered into the computer.

Input Device	=	A device, such as a keyboard, which enables the user to enter information into the computer.
Interface	=	An electronic and physical connection between electrical and electro-mechanical devices, such as that between the central processing unit and the peripheral devices. See also: Serial Interface and Parallel Interface.
IT	=	Information Technology.
Kilobyte	=	1024 Bytes. A measurement of memory capacity.
LAN	=	Local Area Network.
Light-Pen	=	A light sensitive pen which is connected to a computer and can interact with the computer via the screen.
Load	=	To enter a program into a computer memory from a peripheral storage device.
LOGO	=	A high level programming language.
Mainframe computer	=	A large, stationary computer with extensive memory and disk space, capable of performing several different tasks simultaneously.
Menu	=	The list of the choices that are available to the user, usually displayed on the monitor screen, from which selections may be made.
Microcomputer	=	A small portable, single-user computer, usually capable of performing only one task at a time.
Microprocessor	=	An integration circuit performing the functions of a central processor unit.
Minicomputer	=	A computer of medium size, which in terms of memory size and disk space has a capacity between that of a microcomputer and that of a mainframe.
Modem	=	Modulator/ Demodulator. A device capable of converting computer data to a signal that can be transmitted over a telephone line; also capable of reconverting a signal transmitted to a computer via a telephone line to a form that is intelligible to the computer.
On-Line	=	Information that can be accessed directly from a computer.
Output	=	The information reported by the central processing unit to a peripheral device.

Output Device = A peripheral device, such as a printer, which permits the user to receive information from the computer.

Parallel Interface = A type of interface by which information may be transmitted or accepted one computer word at a time.

PASCAL = A highly structured programming language.

PLATO = Programmed Logic for Automatic Teaching Operation. A CAI system available by remote access to any location on the globe.

Prestel = British Telecom's viewdata system.

PROM = Programmable Read Only Memory. A type of ROM that can be programmed by the user, and which cannot be altered or erased once it has been programmed. See also: ROM and EPROM.

RAM = Random Access Memory. A type of computer memory that can be accessed directly.

ROM = Read Only Memory. A type of programmed memory in the computer containing the special instructions for the basic operation of the computer.

Serial Interface = A type of interface by which information may be transmitted or accepted one *bit* at a time. See also: Parallel Interface.

Software = Computer programs, the set of instructions that enable a computer to perform a task or tasks.

Timesharing = The simultaneous use of one computer by several users, generally by means of separate terminals connected to a single computer.

TICCIT = Time-Shared Interactive Computer-Controlled Information Television. A CAI system.

VDU = Visual Display Unit, either a TV set or a monitor.

Bibliography

Abelson, H. (1982), *Apple Logo*. New York: McGraw-Hill.

Adams, J. H./Adams, P. M. (1984), "Computers and French. One Department's Experience", in *Modern Languages in Scotland*, No. 25, pp. 98-102.

Ahmad, K. *et al.* (1985), *Computers, Language Learning and Language Teaching*. Cambridge: Cambridge University Press.

AILA Brussels 84. Proceedings ed. by Jan den Haese/Jos Nivette. Vols. 1-4. Brussels: ITO/VUB.

Albus, J. S. (1981), *Brains, Behavior and Robotics*. New York: McGraw-Hill.

ALLC Bulletin. Association for Literary and Linguistic Computing. Literary and Linguistic Computing Centre, Cambridge.

ALLC Journal. Association for Literary and Linguistic Computing. Literary and Linguistic Computing Centre, Cambridge.

Allen, J. P. B./Davies, Alan, eds. (1977), *The Edinburgh Course in Applied Linguistics*, Vol. 4: *Testing and Experimental Methods*. London: Oxford University Press.

Allen, M. J./Yen, W. M. (1979), *Introduction to Measurement Theory*. Monterey, Ca.: Brooks-Cole Publishing.

Anandam, K. (1976), RSVP. *A Guide for Implementia*. Miami: Dade Community College.

Applied Linguistics. London: Oxford University Press.

Arbid, M. A. (1984), *Computers and the Cybernetic Society*. 2nd ed. Orlando, Florida: Academic Press, Inc.

Astrop, John/Byrne, Donn (1971), *Games for Pairwork*. London: Modern English Publications.

AUDIO-VISUAL Market Place: A Multi-Media Guide (1981). New York: R. R. Bowker Co.

Ayre, P./Hutchings, B./Payne, A. (1980), *Computer Software for Schools*. London: Pitman.

Bacsich, P. D. (1982), *Audio-Videotex Teleconferencing*. Milton Keynes: Open University.

Baker, F. B. (1978), *Computer Managed Instruction*. Englewood Cliffs, N. J.: Educational Technology Publications.

Ball, D./Nash, A. (1982), *An Introduction to Microcomputers in Teaching*. London: Hutchinson.

Barker, P. G. (1982), "Some Experiments in Man-Machine Interaction Relevant to Computer-Assisted Instruction", *British Journal of Educational Technology*, 13, 1, pp. 65-75.

171

Barr, A./Feigenbaum, E., eds. (1981), *The Handbook of Artificial Intelligence*. Los Altos, Ca.: William Kaufmann.

Bates, T. (1982), "Trends in the Use of Audio-Visual Media in Distance Education Systems", in J. S. Daniel *et al. Learning at a Distance*, pp. 8-15.

Beck, I. M./Odeldahl, A. (1977), *Telefonengelska*. Stockholm: Esselte Studium.

Billingsley, J. (1983), *DIY Robotics and Sensors with the BBC Computer*. London: Sunshine Books.

Billingsley, J. (1984), *DIY Robotics and Sensors on the Commodore Computer*. London: Sunshine Books.

Birdsong, David (1977), *Computer-Assisted and Programmed Instruction in Foreign Languages: a selected, annotated bibliography*. Washington, D. C.: Center for Applied Linguistics, ERIC Clearinghouse on Language & Linguistics.

Bradbeer, R./De Bono, P./Laurie, P. (1982), *The Computer Book: An Introduction to Computers and Computing*. London: BBC Publications.

Brain, K./Brain, S. (1984), *Artificial Intelligence on the BBC and Electron*. London: Sunshine Books.

Bramer, M. (1980), "Using computers in distance education: The first ten years of the British Open University", *Computers and Education*, 4, pp. 293-301.

Brazil, D./Coulthard, M./Johns, C. (1980), *Discourse Intonation and Language Teaching*. London: Longman.

Brennan, M./Miller, J. W. (1982), "Making an English language teaching videotape", *ELT Journal*, Vol. 36/3, April; pp. 169-74.

Brims, J. (1979), Camden level crossing: a simulation for language practice. Canterbury: Pilgrims Language Courses.

British Broadcasting Corporation (1978), *Adults learning foreign languages: the role of BBC broadcasting*, by Neil Barnes. London: BBC.

British Broadcasting Corporation (1981), *English by Radio and Television. Using video in the classroom*. London: BBC English by Radio and Television.

British Journal of Educational Technology.

British Journal of Language Teaching.

Broberg, Margareta (1983), "Undervisningsteknologi og fremmedsprogsundervisning", *Tværsproglige blade*, 3. årg. nr. 2. Copenhagen: Danmarks Pædagogiske Bibliotek.

Brown, Erik (1983), *Report of the CILT Computer-Assisted Language Learning Workshop "Assessing Current Programs and Prospects" held at St. Martin's College, Lancaster on 13th and 14th September, 1983*. London: CILT.

Brumfit, C. J. (1981), "Accuracy and fluency: a fundamental distinction for communicative teaching methodology", *Practical English Teacher*, I:3.

Brumfit, C. J. (1984), *Communicative Methodology in Language Teaching: the Roles of Fluency and Accuracy*. Cambridge: Cambridge University Press.

Brumfit, C. J./Johnson, K. (1979), *The Communicative Approach to Language Teaching*. London: Oxford University Press.

Bufe, W./Deichsel, J./Dethloff, U. (1984), *Fernsehen und Fremdsprachenlernen*. Tübingen: Gunter Narr Verlag.

Buscaglia, Michael J./Holman, W. L. (1980), "The Teleprompter: a simulating device for developing communicative competence", *Modern Language Journal*, vol. 64, No. 4, pp. 451-454.

Byrne, D./Rixon, S. (1979), *Communication Games*. Windsor: NFER-Nelson.

Bååth, J. A. (1982), "Experimental Research on Computer-Assisted Distance Education" in J. S. Daniel *et al.* (eds.) *Learning at a Distance*, pp. 303-305.

Bååth, J./Månsson, J.-O. (1977), *CADE - A System for Computer-Assisted Distance Education*. Malmö: Hermods skola.

CAL News. London: Council of Educational Technology.

CALLBOARD: Newsletter on Computer Assisted Language Learning. London: Ealing College.

Calico Journal. Provo, Utah: Brigham Young University Press.

Canale, M./Swain, M. (1980), "Theoretical Bases of Communicative Approaches to Second Language Teaching and Testing", *Applied Linguistics*, I, pp. 1-47.

Candlin, C./Charles, D./Willis, J. (1982), *Video in English Language Teaching: an Inquiry into the Potential Uses of Video Recordings in the Teaching of English as a Foreign Language*. Gosta Green, Birmingham: University of Birmingham, Language Study Unit.

Capron, H. L./Willi, B. K. (1984), *Computers and Data Processing*. 2nd ed. Menlo Park, California: The Benjamin/Cunnings Publishing Co., Inc.

Carroll, Brendan J. (1980), *Testing Communicative Performance: an Interim Study*. Oxford: Pergamon Press.

CET Information Sheets. London: Council of Educational Technology.

CET/MEP Information Sheet: Microelectronics and Special Education. May 1982. London: CET Publications.

CET News. London: Council of Educational Technology.

Chandler, D. (1983), *Exploring English with Microcomputers*. London: Council of Educational Technology.

Chapelle, Carol/Jamieson, Joan (1983), "Language Lessons on the Plato IV System", *System*, Vol. 11, No. 1, pp. 13-20.

Clark, John L. D., ed. (1978), *Direct Testing of Speaking proficiency: Theory and Application: Proceedings of a Two-day Conference*. Princeton, N. J.: Educational Testing Service.

Clark, R./McDonough, J. (1982), *Imaginary Crimes. Materials for Simulation and Role Playing*. Oxford: Pergamon Press.

Clarke, J. D. (1981), *Computer-Assisted Learning of Languages*. Cranfield, England: Cranfield Institute of Technology.

The 1983 Classroom Computer, New Directory of Educational Computer Resources. International Educations Inc., Watertown, Ma.

Clutterbuck, Michael (1979), "The Computer in Foreign Language Teaching", *Babel* (Australia) 15, 1, pp. 33-37.

Coburn, P. *et al.* (1982), *Practical Guide to Computers in Education*. Reading, Mass.: Addison-Wesley Publishing Company.

Collett, M. J. (1980), "Examples of Applications of Computers to Modern Language Study; Part I) The Step-Wise Development of Programs in Reading, Grammar and Vocabulary, *System*, 8, 3, pp. 195-204.

Collett, M. J. (1981), "Examples of Applications of Computers to Modern Language Study; Part II) Storage and retrieval: the Development of an Index of Learning Resources", *System*, 9, 1, pp. 35-40.

Computer Education: A Journal for Teachers interested in Computers and Computing. Computer Education Group, North Staffordshire Polytechnic, Stafford, England.

Computers and Education. Oxford: Pergamon Press.

Computers in Schools. MUSE (Micro Users in Schools and Education). Freepost, Bromsgrove, Worcestershire.

Corder, S. P./Roulet, E., eds. (1973), *Theoretical Linguistics Models in Applied Linguistics.* Paris: Didier.

Coulthard, M. (1977), *An Introduction to Discourse Analysis.* London: Longman.

Cripwell, Ken (1971), *On the Line.* London: Oxford University Press.

Curtis, J./Biedenbach, J., eds. (1979), *Educational Telecommunications Delivery Systems.* 1979. Washington, D. C.

Daniel, J. S./Stroud, M. A./Thompson, J. R., ed. (1982), *Learning at a Distance. A World Perspective.* Edmonton: Athabasca University/International Council for Correspondence Education.

D'Antoni, S. G. (1982), "Videodisc and Videotex: New Media for Distance Education", in J. S. Daniel, *et.al.*, *Learning at a Distance*, pp. 287-90.

Davidsen-Nielsen, N. (1971), Engelsk fonetik. Copenhagen: Gyldendal.

Davies, G./Higgins, J. (1982), *Computers, language and language learning.* London: CILT, Information Guide 22.

Davies, Graham/Steel, David (1981), *First Steps in Computer-Assisted Language Learning at Ealing College of Higher Education.* London: Ealing College.

Davis, Dwight B. (1984), "Supercomputers: a strategic imperative", *High Technology*, Vol. 4, No. 5, pp. 44-52.

Digital: Introduction to Computer-Based Education. Marlborough, Ma.: Digital Equipment Corporation.

Distance Teaching by Cyclops: An Evaluation of the O. Us Telewriting Systems (1982), *JET Paper* Nr. 202. Milton Keynes: The Open University.

Duke, J. (1983), *Interactive Video: implications for education and training. Working Paper* 22. London: Council for Educational Technology.

Dulay, H./Burt, M./Krashen, S. (1982), *Language Two.* New York: Oxford University Press.

Educational Computing. Haywards Heath, Sussex: MAGSUB Ltd.

Educational Technology.

Educational Media International. London: International Council for Educational Media.

van Ek, J. (1975), *The Threshold Level in a European Unit/Credit System for Modern Language Learning by Adults.* Strasbourg: Council of Europe.

van Ek, J. (1976), *Significance of the Threshold Level in the Early Teaching of Modern Languages.* Strasbourg: Council of Europe.

van Ek, J. (1977), *The Threshold Level for Modern Language Learning in Schools.* London: Longman.

van Ek, J./Alexander, L. G. (1975), *Threshold Level English: in a European unit/credit system for modern language learning for adults*. Oxford: Pergamon Press.

Elder, Ron/Wills, R. (1983), *Microcomputers in Primary Education – Using the Microcomputer in the Primary Classroom*. Dundee: Dundee College of Education.

Ellingham, D. (1982), *Managing the Microcomputer in the Classroom. MEP Case Study*, No. 1. London: Council for Educational Technology.

ELT Journal. London: Oxford University Press.

England, Elaine (1981), "The Application of Microcomputers to Teaching English as a Foreign Language". Unpublished MEd. dissertation. University of Wales, Cardiff.

Evans, C. (1979), *The Mighty Micro*. London: Victor Gollancz.

v. Faber, H./Eggers, D., eds. (1980), *Video im Fremdsprachenunterricht*. München: Goethe-Institut.

Fedida, S./Malik, R. (1979), *The Viewdata Revolution*. London: Associated Business Programmes Ltd.

Feigenbaum, E. A./McCorduck, P. (1983), *Artificial Intelligence and Japan's Computer Challenge to the World*. Amsterdam: Addison-Wesley.

Fiddy, P./Wharry, D. (1983), *Microcomputers in Early Education*. London: Longman.

Finocchiaro, Mary/Sako, Sydney (1980), *Foreign Language Testing: a Practical Approach*. New York: Regents Publishing.

Flinck, R. (1978), *Correspondence Education Combined with Systematic Telephone Tutoring*. Malmö: Hermods.

Forester, T. (1980), *The Microelectronics Revolution*. Oxford: Basil Blackwell.

Frick, N./Malmström, S. (1976), *Språkklyftan*. Kristianstad: Tidens förlag.

Friedman, Estelle (1979), *English by Television and Foreign Language Learning*. The Ministry of Education and Culture, Instructional Television Centre, Israel.

Frith, James R., ed. (1980), *Measuring Spoken Language Proficiency*. Washington, DC: Georgetown University Press.

Færch, C./Haastrup, K./Phillipson, R. (1984), *Learner Language and Language Learning*. Copenhagen: Gyldendal and Multilingual Matters Ltd.

Förster, Hans-Peter (1982), *Video-mein Hobby*. München: Humboldt-Taschenbuchverlag.

Förster, Hans-Peter (1983), *Bildschirmtext*. München: Humboldt-Taschenbuchverlag.

Gale, Larrie E. (1983), "Montevidisco: An Anecdotal History of an Interactive Videodisc", in *Calico Journal*, Vol. 1, No. 1, pp. 42-46.

Garland, R., ed. (1982), *Microcomputers and Children in the Primary School*. London: Falmer Press.

Gateway. CET Information Sheet No. 10 (1984). London: Council for Educational Technology.

Geddes, M./Sturtridge, G. (1982), *Video in the Language Classroom*. London: Heinemann.

Gerver, Elisabeth (1984), *Computers and Adult Learning*, Milton Keynes: Open University Press.

Gevarter, W. B. (1982), *An Overview of Artificial Intelligence and Robotics*, Vol. 2: *Robotics*. U. S. Department of Commerce.

Glenn, Allen D./Kehrberg, Kent T. (1981), "The Intelligent Videodisc: An Instructional Tool for the Classroom", *Educational Technology*, October 1981, pp. 60-63.

Gruebel, J./Robinson, W. N./Rutledge, S. (1980), *Directory of Intrastate Educational Telecommunication Systems*. Washington, D. C.

Gruebel, J./Robinson, W. N./Rutledge, S. (1981), "Intrastate Educational Telecommunication Systems: A National Survey", *Educational Technology*, April, pp., 33-36.

Halliday, Michael A. K. (1973), *Explorations in the Functions of Language*. London: Arnold.

Halliday, M./Hassan, R. (1976), *Cohesion in English*. London: Longman.

Harrison, A. (1983), *A Language Testing Handbook*. London: Macmillan.

Hart, R. S. (1981), "Language study and the PLATO system", *Studies in Language Learning*, 3 (1), pp. 3-6.

Hatch, Evelyn M. (1983), *Psycholinguistics. A Second Language Perspective*. Rowley, Mass.: Newbury House.

Hatch, E./Farhady, H. (1982), *Research Design and Statistics for Applied Linguistics*. Rowley, Mass.: Newbury House.

Hawkridge, D. (1983), *New Information Technology in Education*. London: Croom Helm.

Heaton, J. B., ed. (1982), *Language Testing*. Oxford: Modern English Publications.

Helms, H. L., ed. (1983), *The McGraw-Hill Computer Handbook*. New York: McGraw-Hill.

Henderson, John/Humphreys, Fay, eds. (1982), *Audio Visual and Microcomputer Handbook: The SCET Guide to Educational and Training Equipment*. London: Kogan Page.

Herbert, D./Sturtridge, G. (1979), *ELT Guide 2. Simulations*. London: English Language Teaching Institute, The British Council.

Higgins, John (1982), "Computers in Language Training", *Language Training*, No. 3, pp. 3-6.

Higgins, John (1982), *Grammarland: A Non-Directive Use of the Computer in Language Learning*. London: The British Council.

Higgins, John (1982), "How Real is a Computer Simulation?", *ELT Documents*, 113, pp. 102-109.

Higgins, John (1982), "The Use of the Computer in English Language Teaching", *CILT Information Guide*, 22.

Higgins, J./Johns, T. (1984), *Computers in Language Learning*. London: Collins Educational.

Hill, Brian (1981), "Some Applications of media technology to the teaching and learning of languages", *Language Teaching and Linguistics: Abstracts*, Vol. 14, No. 3, 1981, pp. 147-161.

Hockey, Susan (1980), *A Guide to Computer Applications in the Humanities*. Baltimore and London: Johns Hopkins University Press.

Holden, Susan (1981), *Drama in Language Teaching*. Harlow: Longman.

Holec, H. (1980), *Autonomy and Foreign Language Learning*. Strasbourg: Council of Europe.

176

Holmberg, B. (1981), *Status and Trends of Distance Education*. London: Kogan Page.

Holmberg, B. (1982), *Recent Research into Distance Education*. Hagen: FernUniversität.

Holmes, Glyn/Kidd, Marilyn E. (1982), "Second Language Learning and Computers", *The Canadian Modern Language Review*, Vol. 38, No. 3, pp. 503-513.

Hooper, R. (1983), "The computer as a medium for distance education", in J. Megarry *et al.* (1983), *World Yearbook of Education 1982/83*, pp. 103-108.

Howe, J. A. M. (1981), "Artificial Intelligence and Computer-Assisted Learning: Ten Years On". *Selected Readings in Computer-Based Learning*, N. J. Rushby, ed., pp. 101-112.

Howe, J. A. M./Ross, P. M., eds. (1981), *Micocomputers in Secondary Education: Issues and Techniques*. London: Kogan Page.

Hudson, L./Bunting, D. (1982), "The Telenetwork System: A Viable Alternative for Delivering Distant Instruction", *Educational Technology*, August, pp. 17-19.

Humanistiske Data 3-83 (1983). NAVFs EDB-senter for humanistisk forskning, Norges Almenvitenskapelige Forskningsråd. Bergen, Norway.

Hurly, P. (1982), "Using Videotex in Distance Education", in J. S. Daniel, *et al.*, *Learning at a Distance*, p. 109.

ICAME News. The Norwegian Centre for the Humanities. Bergen, Norway.

ILEA Educational Computing Newsletter. Computers Inspectorate, Inner London Education Authority, County Hall, London.

Illingworth, Valerie, ed., with Glaser, Ted/Pyle, Ian (1983), *Dictionary of Computing*. Oxford: Oxford Scientific Books.

Jacobson, H M./ Zettersten, A. (1985), *En bruksanvisning till lektionsgenerator för språkträning på mikrodator*. Lund: Studentlitteratur AB.

Jamieson, Joan/Chapelle, Carol (1982), "ESL on the PLATO System". Computer-Assisted Instruction: Special Issue of *English for Specific Purposes*, 58/59, pp. 3-6.

Johansen, /McNulty, /McNeal, (1978), *Electronic Education: Using Teleconferencing in Postsecondary Organizations*.

Johansson, S./Tysdahl, B. J. (1981), *Papers from the First Conference for English Studies*, Oslo, 17-19 September, 1980.

Johns, Tim (1982), "CAL for English Teaching", *CALNEWS*, 18, pp. 4-5.

Johns, Tim (1982), *Exploratory CAL: an alternative use of the computer in teaching foreign languages*. Birmingham, English for Overseas Students Unit, University of Birmingham.

Johns, Tim (1982) "The Uses of an Analytic Generator: the computer as Teacher of English for Specific Purposes", *ELT Documents*, 112, pp. 96-105 (1982).

Johnson, Keith (1982), *Communicative Syllabus Design and Methodology*. Oxford: Pergamon Press.

Johnson, Keith/Morrow, Keith, eds. (1981), *Communication in the Classroom*. London: Longman.

Jones, Chris (1981), *Computers and Testing*. London: The British Council.

Jones, Chris (1983), "Computer assisted language learning: testing or teaching?" *ELT Journal*, Vol. 37/3, July 1983, pp. 247-250.

Jones, Ken (1978), *Simulations in Language Teaching*. Cambridge: Cambridge University Press.

Jones, R. (1980), *Microcomputers: Their Uses in Primary Schools*. London: Council of Educational Technology.

Jones, R.L./Spolsky, B., eds. (1975), *Testing Language Proficiency*. Washington, DC: Center for Applied Linguistics.

Journal of Computer-Based Instruction. Association for the Development of Computer-Based Instructional Systems, Minneapolis.

Jung, Udo, ed. (1985), *Man and the Media*. Proceedings of the AILA Symposium at Frankfurt, June 12-15, 1984.

Kenning, M. J./Kenning, M.-M. (1981), "Computer-Assisted Language Teaching Made Easy", *British Journal of Language Teaching*, 19, 3, pp. 119-23, and p. 136.

Kenning, M. J./Kenning, M.-M. (1984), *An Introduction to Computer Assisted Language Teaching*. London: Oxford University Press.

Kirman, J. M./Goldberg, J. (1981), "Distance Education: Teacher Training Via Live Television and Concurrent Group Telephone Conferencing", *Educational Technology*, April, pp. 41-42.

Kleppin, Karin (1980), *Das Sprachlernspiel im Fremdsprachenunterricht: Untersuchungen zum Lehrer und Lernerverhalten im Sprachlernspiel*. Tübingen: Gunter Narr Verlag.

Knapp-Potthoff, A./Knapp, K. (1982), *Fremdsprachenlernen und -lehren*. Stuttgart: Kohlhammer.

Krashen, S. (1981), *Second Language Acquisition and Second Language Learning*. Oxford: Pergamon Press.

Krashen, S. (1982), *Principles and Practice in Second Language Acquisition*. Oxford: Pergamon Press.

Krashen, S./Terrell, T. (1983), *The Natural Approach*. Oxford: Pergamon Press.

Krutch, J. (1981), *Experiments in Artificial Intelligence*. Indianapolis: Howard W. Sams.

Kühlwein, W./Raasch, A., eds. (1984), *Bildschirmtext. Perspektiven eines neuen Mediums*. Tübingen: Gunter Narr Verlag.

Lado, R. (1961), Language Testing: *The Construction and Use of Foreign Language Tests*. London: Longman.

Language Teaching: The International Abstracting Journal for Language Teachers and Applied Linguistics. Cambridge: Cambridge University Press.

Last, R. W. (1984), *Language Teaching and the Micro*. Oxford: Basil Blackwell.

Lavery, M. (1981), *Active Viewing: Video Exploitation Techniques in the Language Learning Classroom*. Canterbury: Pilgrims Publications.

Leather, Jonathan, ed. (1980), *Computers in Language Teaching: Synopses of Papers Presented during a Conference at the Polytechnic of Central London 27 June, 1980*. London School of Languages, Polytechnic of Central London.

Lee, W. R. (1979), *Language-Teaching Games and Contests*. 2nd. ed. Oxford: Oxford University Press.

Leech, G./Candlin, C., eds. (1985), *The Computer and the English Language*. Harlow: Longman.

Lewis, B./Tagg, D., eds. (1981), *Computers in Education*. Amsterdam: North Holland.

Lewis, E. G./Massad, C. E. (1975), *The Teaching of English as a Foreign Language in Ten Countries*. Stockholm: Almqvist & Wiksell.

Lian, A. P./Russel, R./Joy, B. K. (1982), *Introduction to Computer-Assisted Second Language Education*. Massey University, Australia.

Livingstone, Carol (1983), *Role Play in Language Learning*. Harlow: Longman.

Lonergan, J. (1984), *Video in Language Teaching*. Cambridge: Cambridge University Press.

Longley, D./Shain, M. (1982), *Dictionary of Information Technology*. London: Mac-Millan.

Luehrmann, A./Peckham, H./Ramirez, M. (1982), *A First Course in Computing*. New York: McGraw-Hill.

Madden, J. (1979). *Videotex in Canada*. Ottawa: Ministry of Supply and Services.

Maddison, A. (1982), *Microcomputers in the Classroom*. Sevenoaks, Kent: Hodder & Stoughton Educational.

Maddison, J. (1983), *Education in the Microelectronics Era*. Milton Keynes: Open University Press.

Maley, A. (1983), "New lamps for old: realism and surrealism in foreign language teaching", *ELT Journal*, Vol. 37/4, October, pp. 295-303.

Maley, Alan/Duff, Alan (1978), *Drama Techniques in Language Learning*. Cambridge: Cambridge University Press.

Malone, L./Johnson, J. (1981), *BASIC Discoveries*. Palo Alto, Ca.: Creative Publications.

Martin, J. (1982), *Viewdata and the Information Society*. Hemel Hempstead: Prentice/Hall International.

McDonough, S. H. (1981), *The Psychology of Foreign Language Learning*. London: George Allen and Unwin.

McGovern, J., ed. (1983), *Video Applications in Language Teaching*. Oxford: Pergamon Press.

Media in Education and Development, A Journal of the British Council, December 1983.

Megarry, Jacquetta (1977), *Aspects of Simulation & Gaming*. An Anthology of SAGSET Journal Volumes 1-4. London: Kogan Page.

Megarry, J., *et al.* (1983), *World Yearbook of Education 1982/83: Computers and Education*. London: Kogan Page.

MEP Information Sheets. Newcastle upon Tyne: Microelectronics Education Programme.

Meredith, M. D./Briggs, B. I. (1982), *Bigtrak Plus*. London: Council for Educational Technology.

Micro et Robots. Paris: La Société des Publications Radio – Electriques et Scientifiques.

Molnar, A. R. (1983), "Intelligent videodisc and the learning society", *Journal of Computer Based Instruction*, 6, pp. 11-16.

Moore, M. (1981), "Educational Telephone Networks", *Teaching at a Distance*, 19, pp. 29-31.

Nash, A./Ball, D. (1982), *An Introduction to Microcomputers in Teaching*. London: Hutchinson.

Nilsson, J. (1983), *Integrerad text-TV i utbildningsradio*. Stockholm: Sveriges utbildningsradio.

Noss, R. (1983), *Starting LOGO*. Hatfield: AUCBE.

Oates, Wiliam (1981), "An Evaluation of Computer-Assisted Instruction for English Grammar Review", The PLATO System and Language Study. Complete issue of *Studies in Language Learning*, University of Illinois, 3, 1, pp. 193-200.

Obrist, A. J. (1983), *The Microcomputer and the Primary School*. London: Hodder and Stoughton.

Odor, P./Entwistle, N. (1982), *The Introduction of Microelectronics into Education*. Edinburgh: Scottish Academic Press.

Olgren, C. H./Parker, L. A. (1983), *Teleconferencing, Technology and Application*. Dedham MA: Artech House Inc.

Oller, J. W., Jr. (1979), *Language Tests at School: a Pragmatic Approach*. London: Longman.

Oller, J. W., Jr., ed. (1981), *Issues in Language Testing Research*. Rowley, Mass.: Newbury House.

Oller, J. W., Jr./Perkins, K., eds. (1980), *Research in Language Testing*. Rowley, Mass.: Newbury House.

OLS Newsletter. Newsletter about Open Learning Systems. Sponsored by the Council for Educational Technology and the Scottish Council for Educational Technology. Southampton.

Omaggio, Alice C. (1979), *Games and Simulations in the Foreign Language Classroom*. Arlington, Va.: Center for Applied Linguistics, ERIC Clearinghouse on Languages and Linguistics.

Open Learning. CET Information Sheet no. 5 (March 1984). London: Council for Educational Technology.

Oskarsson, Mats (1980), *Approaches to Self-Assessment in Foreign Language Learning*. Prepared for the Council of Europe by Mats Oskarsson. New. ed. Oxford, New York: Pergamon Press for and on behalf of the Council of Europe Modern Languages Project.

O'Shea, T./Self, J. (1983), *Learning and Teaching with Computers*. Brighton: The Harvester Press.

Otto, Frank (1980), "Computer-Assisted Instruction in Language Teaching and Learning", *Annual Review of Applied Linguistics*, pp. 58-59.

Owen, Kenneth, ed. (1982), *Videotex in Education: a new technology briefing*. London: Council for Educational Technology.

Palmer, A./Rodgers, T. S. (1979), "Games in Language Teaching", *Simulations*, ELT Guide -2. London: NFER Publishing Co.

Papert, S. (1980), *Breakthroughs: Astonishing Advances in Medicine, Science and Technology*. Boston: Houghton Miffin Company.

180

Papert, S. (1980), *Mindstorms: Children, Computers and Powerful Ideas*. Brighton: The Harvester Press.

Parker, L. A./Monson, M. K. (1980), *Teletechniques: An Instructional Model for Interactive Teleconferencing*. Englewood Cliffs, N. J.

Parker, L. A./Riccomini, B., eds. (1977), *The Telephone in Education*. Madison, Wisconsin.

Perker, Sibyl B., ed. (1984), *Encyclopedia of Electronics and Computers*. New York: McGraw-Hill.

Payne, A./Hutchings, B./Ayre, P. (1980), *Computer Software* for Schools. London: Pitman Education Ltd.

Passe, Jeff (1984), "Phil Donahue: An Excellent Model for Leading a Discussion", in *Journal of Teacher Education*, Vol. XXXV, No. 1, Jan.-Febr. 1984, pp. 43-48.

Personal Computer World. London: Sportscene Publishers (PCW) Ltd.

Phillips, M. K. (1983), "J. R. Firth as computational linguist: a description of the GLOC test analysis software package in its linguistics context". Amplified version of a talk given at London University Institute of Education, 9 February 1983.

Phillips, M. K. (1983), "The microcomputer and ESP-purposes, programs and priorities". To appear in *Espmena bulletin*.

Pilbeam, A. (1982), "Other Uses of Computers in Language Teaching: an aid in writing materials", *Language Training*, Vol. 3, o. 4, 1982.

Poirot, J. L. (1980), *Computers and Education*. Sterling Swift: Texas.

Post, Nancy E. (1982), "Introducing Computer-Assisted Instruction into an ESL/ESP Curriculum". Computer-Assisted Instruction. Special issue of *English for Specific Purposes*, 58/59 (1982), pp. 10-11.

Poulter, Virgil L. (1969), "Computer-Assisted Laboratory Testing", *Modern Language Journal*, 53, 8, pp. 561-64.

Proceedings of the International Symposium on Language Testing, Hong Kong, 19-21 December, 1982. Oxford: Pergamon Press (1985).

Putnam, C. E. (1981), "Technology and Foreign Language Teaching", *British Journal of Language Teaching*, 19, 2, pp. 63-68.

Putnam, C. E. (1983), "Foreign Language Instructional Technology: The State of Art", in *Calico Journal*, Vol. 1, No. 1, pp. 35-41.

Rich, Elaine (1983), *Artificial Intelligence*. New York: McGraw-Hill.

Richards, J. C./Schmidt, R. W. (1983), *Language and Communication*. London: Longman.

Rietmann, Kearney (1981), "Adding Sight and Sound to Computer-Assisted Instruction: Interactive Video", *World Language English*, 1, 1, pp. 43-45.

Rivers, Wilga (1981), *Teaching Foreign Language Skills*. 2nd ed.

Rixon, Shelagh (1981), *How to use games in Language Teaching*. London: Macmillan.

Roach, Peter (1981), *The Microcomputer as an Aid in Pronunciation Teaching*. Leeds: Dept. of Linguistics and Phonetics, University of Leeds.

Roberts, J. T. (1982), "Recent developments in ELT", Part I and Part II, *Language Teaching*, April 1982, pp. 94-110, July 1982, pp. 174-94.

Ruggles, R. *et al.* (1982), "Videodiscs: Will Laser Technology Help Light the Way for Learning at a Distance", in Daniel, J. S., *etal. Learning at a Distance.*

Ruggles, R. H. *et al.* (1982), *Learning at a Distance and the New Technology.* Vancouver: Educational Research Institute of British Columbia.

Rushby, N. J. (1979), *An Introduction to Educational Computing.* London: Croom Helm.

Rushby, N. J., ed. (1981), *Selected Readings in Computer-Based Learning.* London: Kogan Page.

Ryback, S. (1980), *Learning languages from the BBC: research into courses.* London: BBC.

Self, J. (1985), *Microcomputers in Education.* Brighton: The Harvester Press.

Sherrington, Richard (1973), *Television and Language Skills.* London: Oxford University Press.

Sigel, E., ed. (1980), *Video Discs: The Technology, the Applications and the Future.* White Plains, New York: Knowledge Industry Publications, Inc.

Sigel, E. *et al.* (1980), *Videotext: The Coming Revolution in Home/Office Information Retrieval.* White Plains, New York: Knowledge Industry Publications, Inc.

Sigurd, B. (1982), "Commentator: a computer model of verbal production", *Linguistics* 20, pp. 611-32.

Sinclair, J. M./Coulthard, M. (1975), *Towards an analysis of discourse: the English used by teachers and pupils.* London: Oxford University Press.

Smith, C. (1982), *Microcomputer in Education.* London: Ellis Harwood/John Wiley.

Smith, P. R. (1981), *Computer Assisted Learning.* Oxford: Pergamon Press.

Smith, P. W. *et al.* (1981), *A CAL Software Library Manual.* London: Schools Council/Chelsea College.

Spolsky, Bernard, ed. (1978), *Approaches to Language Testing.* Washington, DC: Center for Applied Linguistics.

Spolsky, Bernard, ed. (1979), *Some Major Tests.* Washington, DC: Center for Applied Linguistics.

Spolsky, Bernard, ed. (1978, 1979), *Advances in language testing research series: 1 and 2.* Washington, DC: Center for Applied Linguistics.

Stewart, D. (1984), "Fibre optics", *Practical Electronics,* July, pp. 42-46.

Strevens, P. (1980), *Teaching English as an International Language – from practice to principle.* Oxford: Pergamon Press.

System, the International Journal of Educational Technology and Language Learning Systems. Oxford: Pergamon Press.

System 1983. February. Special issue on microcomputers.

Teleconferencing. CET Information Sheet No. 7 (October 1983). London: Council for Educational Technology.

Teleconferencing and Electronic Communication. Vol. I (1982), Vol II (1983). University of Wisconsin: Center for Interactive Programs.

Telesoftware. CET Information Sheet No. 3 (November 1982). London: Council for Educational Technology.

Thomas, J. L., ed. (1981), *Microcomputers in the Schools.* Phoenix, Arizona: The Onyx Press.

Thompson, G. (1984), "The Development of the Educational Telephone Network at the University of Wisconsin", *ICDE, International Council for Distance Education,* Vol. 5, pp. 47-52.

Thompson, V. (1982), *Prestel and Education: a report of a one year trial.* London: Council for Educational Technology.

Thompson, V. *et al.* (1982), *Videotex in Education: a new technology briefing.* London: Council for Educational Technology.

Thorén, F. (1967), *10.000 ord för tio års engelska.* Lund: Gleerups.

Tydeman, J. *et al.* (1982), *Teletext and Videotext in the United States: Market, Potential, Technology.* New York: McGraw-Hill.

The Use of Brodcast Material in Language Teaching (1980), A special edition of Volume 18, Nos. 2 & 3 of the *British Journal of Language Teaching.*

USPEC. London: Council of Educational Technology.

USPEC 32 (1980), *A Guide to the Selection of Microcomputers.* London: CET Publications.

Valette, R. M. (1977), *Modern Language Testing.* 2nd ed. New York: Harcourt, Brace Jovanovich. Inc.

Veith, R. H. (1983), *Television's Teletext.* New York: North-Holland.

Videotex Systems. USPEC 32 d (March 1984). London: Council for Educational Technology.

Watcyn-Jones, P. (1978), *Act English.* Harmondsworth: Penguin.

Watson, J./Hill, A. (1984), *A Dictionary of Communication and Media Studies.* London: Edward Arnold Ltd.

Watt, D. (1983), *Learning with LOGO.* New York: McGraw-Hill.

Watt, D. (1984), *Learning with Commodore LOGO.* New York: McGraw-Hill.

Wegner, H. (1977), *Feature films in second language instruction.* Arlington, Va: Center for Applied Linguistics.

Weizenbaum, J. (1984), *Computer Power and Human Reason. From Judgment to Calculation.* Harmondsworth, Middlesex: Penguin Books Ltd.

Wells, Gordon (1981), *Learning Through Interaction. The Study of Language Development.* Cambridge: Cambridge University Press.

Widdowson, H. G. (1973), "Directions in the teaching of discourse", in Corder, S. P./Roulet, E., eds., *Theoretical Linguistics Models in Applied Linguistics.*

Widdowson, H. G. (1978), *Teaching Language as Communication.* London: Oxford University Press.

Wilkins, David A. (1976), *Notional syllabuses: a taxonomy and its relevance to foreign language curriculum development.* London: Oxford University Press.

Winograd, Terry (1972), *Understanding Natural Language.* New York: Academic Press.

Winograd, Terry (1983), *Language as a Cognitive Process.* Vol. I: Syntax. Reading, Mass.: Addison-Wesley.

Winston, P. (1984), *Artificial Intelligence.* 2nd ed. Amsterdam: Addison-Wesley.

Wright, Andrew/Betterridge, David/Buckby, Michael (1979), *Games for Language Learning.* Cambridge: Cambridge University Press.

Wyatt, David H. (1982), "Computer-Assisted Instruction: Individualised Learning in ESL/ESP". Computer-Assisted Instruction. Special issue of *English for Specific Purposes*, (Oregon), 58/59, pp. 1-3.

Wyatt, David H. (1983), "Computer-Assisted Language Instruction: Present State and Future Prospects", *System*, Vol. 11, No. 1, pp. 3-11.

Zettersten, A. (1969), *A Statistical Study of the Graphic System of Present-Day American English*. Lund: Studentlitteratur AB.

Zettersten, A. (1969), *A Word-Frequency List of Scientific English*. Lund: Studentlitteratur AB.

Zettersten, A. (1978), *A Word-Frequency List Based on American Press Reportage*. Publications of the Department of English, University of Copenhagen. Vol. 6. Copenhagen: Akademisk forlag.

Zettersten, A. (1979), *Experiments in English Vocabulary Testing*. Malmö: Liber.

Zettersten, A. "Experiments on Large-Scale Vocabulary Testing", Proceedings of the International Symposium on Language Testing. Hong Kong 19-21 December, 1982. Oxford: Pergamon Press (1985).

Zettersten, A. (1983), "Experiment med nya Teknologier i Språkundervisningen: Mikrodator, Teledata, Text-TV och Video", in *Lingva* 3/83, pp. 124-129.

Zettersten, A. (1983), *Business in Hong Kong. How to make your own video programme*. An Exercise in Business English. Based on a functional/notional approach". Copenhagen: TV/AV afdelingen – Department of English, University of Copenhagen.

Zettersten, A. (1985), "Language training and testing by means of new electronic media", in Jung, U. (ed.), *Man and the Media*.

Zettersten, A./Jacobson, M. (1986), *How to use an authoring program*. Lund: Studentlitteratur AB.

Zettersten, A./Jacobson, M. (1985), *Brainlearn*. A system for English Language Learning by Microcomputer including authoring programs. Lund: Studentlitteratur AB.

Zettersten, A./Lundman, S. (1982-84), *Engelsk grammatik. Programvara för ABC-datorer*. Grundskolan: Del 1-8. Gymnasieskolan: Del 1-8. Stockholm: Liber.

Zettersten, A./Lundman, S. (1984), *Basengelska 1-4*. Norrköping: Statens skola för vuxna and Lund: Studentlitteratur AB.

Zuber-Skerrit, O., ed. (1983), *Video in Higher Education*. London: Kogan Page.

Index

language testing   10, 126, 156, 157
LANS   150
large-scale vocabulary testing   126
laser-based videodisc   82
laser-beams   123
learning   15
learning package   102
learning system   146
lesson driver   40
lesson generator   159
light pen   21
"Linking Up"   161
listening comprehension   142, 143, 148
"The Living City"   68, 72
LOGO   97, 98
LSP   12, 52, 114, 118, 119, 120, 121

magneto-optical videodiscs   83
MAIL   145
mainframe computer   9, 21, 92, 126, 141
"Making a Fianze"   87
mean score   129
media-mix   122, 148
Micro TICCIT   21
microchip revolution   9
microcomputer   9, 10, 20, 32, 35, 39, 90, 92, 93, 126, 136, 146, 150, 152, 153, 156, 158
microcomputer revolution   13, 74
microcomputer/video interface   78, 157
Microplato   21
minicomputer   9, 21
modem   43
moderation   87
modules   16
monitor   17
"Monopoly"   88
"Montevidisco"   83, 89
multi-media approach   115
multi-media courses   98, 148, 149, 158
multi-media system   21, 83, 123
multiple-choice test   21, 28, 32, 128, 131
multiple choice vocabulary test   66, 131, 132

national comparison   129, 130

National Swedish Telecommunications Services   43
networks   150
norm-oriented language teaching   15

Open University   145
optical fibres   123, 124, 150, 151, 157
optical scanner   128
optical videodisc   83
ORACLE   62
oral production   16, 142
OUTNET   122
overhead projector transparency   148

"Panorama of the Week"   62, 63, 72, 101
pattern recognition   92
performance   15, 16
performance analysis   16
performance-oriented language teaching   15
personal computer   146
PLATO   21, 146, 157
Prestel   12, 43, 51, 146
Prestel Gateway   51
proficiency levels   142, 143
programmed teaching   13
pronunciation   78, 142
pronunciation exercises   36

question-answer dialogue   28

R (P-BIS)   129
radio   101, 114, 124, 149, 150, 156
radiovision   101, 114
random access   21, 36, 82, 83, 156
reinforcement   62, 66, 118, 150
robot   10, 92, 93, 96, 97, 157
role-playing   85, 87, 157
RSVP   142

satellite communication   118
satellites   12, 101, 122, 153, 157
scorability   131
score   129
scoring   126
second generation   20
"Seeing a Doctor in China"   87
self-assessment   135